German Design 1870-1918

JOHN HESKETT

German Design
1870-1918

Taplinger Publishing Company
New York

First published in the United States 1986 by
TAPLINGER PUBLISHING CO., INC.
New York, New York

ISBN 0-8008-3208-6

For Reni, with love

Printed and bound in Great Britain

Contents

Acknowledgements

In preparing the text and illustrations many people have been of assistance. I would particularly like to thank Georg Buchner of Darmstadt for his help and friendship, Dr Helmut Drubba of Hannover for many kindnesses over many years, and Dr Pat Kirkham of Leicester for generously sending me material discovered in her own researches. The library staff at Ravensbourne College of Design and Communication and at Sheffield City Polytechnic's Faculty of Art and Design have been exceedingly generous with their time and assistance. Frau Dr Zischka and Frau Springer of the Munich Stadtmuseum and Ivars Alksnis and Peter Pirkl of Geneva provided invaluable help in obtaining illustrations. My secretary at Ravensbourne, Viv Haslam, not only typed the manuscript in its varied manifestations, but provided superbly efficient support at crucial times. At home, my wife and children held the fort during absences researching, and patiently tolerated the long silences whilst writing. To adequately thank everyone who deserves it would require a long list, but the absence of individual mention does not mean my gratitude is any the less.

The German Empire 1871-1918

DENMARK

Kiel.

HOLSTEIN

.Rostock

POMERANIA

Königsberg.

Danzig.

PRUSSIA

.Lübeck

.Hamburg

.Bremen

Weser

HANOVER

.Hanover

.Berlin

Posen.

POLAND

NETHERLANDS

WESTPHALIA

Elbe

BRANDENBURG

POSEN

.Dortmund

Krefeld.

.Düsseldorf

.Göttingen

.Breslau

.Wuppertal

Kassel.

.Leipzig

SILESIA

.Solingen

BELGIUM

.Cologne

Aachen.

Weimar.

Dresden.

Koblenz.

HESSE

SAXONY

LUXEMBURG

.Frankfurt

Mainz.

.Hanau

Prague.

Darmstadt.

SAARLAND

Rhine

.Metz

ALSACE

LORRAINE

.Heilbron

.Nuremburg

AUSTRIA

.Strasbourg

.Stuttgart

FRANCE

.Ulm

BAVARIA

BADEN

WÜRTTEMBURG

.Munich

.Constance

Zurich.

SWITZERLAND

	Alsace Lorraine annexed from France 1871.
	Boundary of German Empire 1871.

Introduction

Until 1870, Germany was a geographical expression for an expanse of territory divided into numerous independent states, of which Prussia emerged in the first half of the nineteenth century as the largest in area and, in military and political terms, the most potent. In that year, after careful manipulation by the Prussian Chancellor, Otto von Bismark, a coalition army from the German states under Prussian leadership went to war with France and gained a complete and stunning victory, the catalyst for unification in 1871. The new German Empire rapidly developed a powerful and aggressive nationalism which, in the visual arts, was manifested in the search for a national style capable of expressing the newfound sense of unity. This concept of style was essentially historical in nature, based on a retrospective recognition of the collective features which constituted a distinctive style, and in common with the rest of Europe at that time, directed towards the revival of past styles, rather than the creation of new ones. The relevance of this approach was increasingly called into question, however, as new technical forms proliferated, providing a challenge to accepted concepts of art in everyday life. Such innovative forms were the material expression of profound changes in German life, as a rapid growth in industrialization, population and urbanization transformed production and consumption at home, the role of exports in the national economy, and indeed, the whole pattern of social life in Germany.

By 1900, Germany ranked with Britain and the USA as a leading industrial power in the world, and attempts to define a national style evolved into a broad, many-faceted movement for cultural reform, embodied in a variety of organizations, theories and practice seeking appropriate expression for experience of contemporary life. Whilst craft influences remained strong, and attempts to conserve or restore elements of traditional life and culture found many adherents, what was remarkable about Germany in the early twentieth century was the range of ideas and practice seeking to reconcile art and industry as an expression of contemporary national culture.

Probably the best known, and certainly the most extensively researched manifestation of this tendency, is the organization known as the German *Werkbund,* which was an essential link in the thesis of Nikolaus Pevsner's book, *Pioneers of Modern Design,* that, more than any other, has shaped attitudes to this period. It depicted modern design as emerging from a line of development originating in Victorian England, through Pugin, Ruskin, Morris and the Arts and Crafts Movement, via the *Werkbund* to the culminating point of the so-called Modern Movement epitomised by the *Bauhaus* in Germany. The purpose of *Pioneers* was to identify the origins and celebrate the existence of the Modern Movement, and to do so the evidence mustered in the original edition of 1936 was highly selective. The most fundamental criticism of Pevsner's methodology relates to his teleological approach, looking to history to justify a particular view of the present. Based essentially on aesthetic premises, without delving into the complexities of contextual influences and relationships, *Pioneers* imposed a linear interpretation upon an age that was diverse and plural in nature, taking part of a complex picture and representing it as the only significant element.

Whatever one's reservations about Pevsner's approach, however, the fact remains that his research into the history of design was itself pioneering, and informed by a deep conviction of the importance of design. His interpretation was extraordinarily influential, was for many years definitive, and has only come into question in the last decade.

To fully examine this phenomenon and argue other possibilities goes far beyond the subject of this book and the scope of this introduction. What is relevant here, and is a surprising aspect of Pevsner's work and legacy, is the extent to which developments in nineteenth century German applied art and design were dealt with, at best, cursorily, and in many cases, not at all. This is the more remarkable if one recalls that he grew up and was educated in that country. In contrast, he did more than anyone to alert the British public to the achievements and value of their Victorian heritage and his emphasis on the impact of the British example abroad was essentially correct, and was indeed powerfully influential. So too were ideas and developments he identified from other sources, such as Paris, Vienna and Chicago. Yet when he refers to events in Germany, it is only from around the turn of the century, and in terms of an argument that looks forward to the 1920s. The late nineteenth century in Germany, the culture into which Pevsner was born in 1902, was virtually ignored. In nothing else, perhaps, was he more typical of the followers of the German Modern Movement than in rejecting the age which preceded it, and, it can be argued, decisively shaped it.

The significance of an age, however, cannot be assessed primarily by its relevance to later events, for each has a character and meaning of its own. Essentially, therefore, the purpose of this book is an attempt to redress the balance: to consider the period of the German Empire in its own terms and not as an antecedent to the avant-garde of the 1920s; to acknowledge the range of German developments as well as influences from other countries; and to place the evolution of applied art and design in Germany in a broad context of contemporary events and thought, with aesthetic concerns considered as part of a general historical process. The treatment is basically chronological, but I hope within it to deal with some of the paradoxes that existed, such as visions of the future created from illusions of the past, attempts to reconcile individual creativity to the demands of a paternalistic society and autocratic state, or the efforts of individual artists to assert themselves as the high priests of modern industrial civilization and consciousness. There are particular problems in writing on the subject of another country, whose language may have layers of meaning not easily susceptible to accurate translation. Where this is so, I have attempted to explain the term in question and have used it untranslated. In addition, where the title of a movement or organization is commonly used in untranslated form, I have again used the original. In such cases, German terms and titles are printed in italics. Unless otherwise acknowledged, all translations of quoted texts are my own.

JOHN HESKETT

1 The Unification of Germany

On January 18th 1871, during the Franco-Prussian War, whilst the German coalition forces under Prussian leadership besieged Paris, a ceremony was held in the *Galérie des Glaces* at the Palace of Versailles to proclaim the foundation of the Second German Empire, with the King of Prussia as its Emperor. The newly unified state was to have an eventful lifespan of seventy-five years. Founded on the successful application of Bismark's doctrine of 'blood and iron', it eventually foundered in a welter of blood and ruin in 1945.

In an important respect that end was predicated in its beginning, for the ceremony at Versailles was overwhelmingly military in tone, aptly reflecting the reality that co-operation in a successful war had been the catalyst for unification, so realizing a long-held dream for many Germans. It had been the focus of republican and democratic aspirations in the revolutions of 1848, though now the autocratic forces which repressed those efforts in order to preserve their own power, handed unification from above to the German people. However, the irony of the situation was lost in the celebration of the event, as chauvinistic fervour created a powerful if fleeting social unity. Popular enthusiasm for the war against an old enemy reached ecstatic heights as success in battle led swiftly to an overwhelming victory, which was carefully manipulated to maintain the hegemony of Prussia in the new Empire.

A more tangible influence contributing to unification was the process of industrialization, which had rapidly accelerated since the 1850s and provided the foundation-stone of Prussia's swift rise to supremacy in Germany. The Prussian tradition of subordinating all aspects of national life to the requirements of state, moreover, meant the development of key industries became heavily influenced by military policy, with, for example, railway lines built by private companies being laid on routes specified by the Army. As a junior officer, the Prussian Chief of Staff in the war, Field Marshall Moltke, had studied railways as an instrument of strategic manoeuvre, and his mastery in using them to deploy troops had been decisive. The war also revealed serious problems in the system, however, which subsequently had a profound impact on railway policy and design. Specialization in armaments-production by particular companies also bore fruit in the war, as with the steel, breech-loading field-guns by Krupp of Essen, which had far greater range than comparable French artillery, giving a tactical advantage that was used to devastating effect.

Autocracy, militarism and nationalism were therefore confirmed by the achievement of unification and continued to influence German society and culture, including design, as they developed after 1871 through to the period of National Socialism. Some historians interpret this continuity as leading, almost inevitably, to the rise of Hitler. [1] To subordinate interpretations of modern German history to the extent it contributed to the Third Reich, may represent a necessary attempt to explain the incomprehensible, but it nevertheless opens the way for serious distortions. It ignores the specific conditions and consciousness of the pre-Hitler period and, moreover, by emphasising uniquely German traits, tends to underplay influences and ideas from other countries and, indeed, the diversity which existed within the German context.

Elements of continuity certainly existed, though not unchallenged, for innovation was both stimulated and given wider scope by unification, with industrialization and a rapidly increasing population becoming concentrated in overcrowded manufacturing centres, changing the social map of Germany. Urbanization brought new forms of consciousness, evident in the spread of radical political ideas and new, provocative forms of cultural expression. This process of change provoked a constant sense of crisis, since it occurred within a rigidly hierarchical social framework, but there was not simply a polar antagonism between the forces of authority and the agents of change, rather a more complex scenario in which both became interwoven and interdependent. For example, in Bismarck, first the Prussian and then Imperial Chancellor, Germany had one of the greatest statesmen of the age to shape its policies. His overriding purpose, however, was to preserve the existing order, and to achieve this he constantly appropriated change and innovation from any quarter to pre-empt radical influences. To the same end, the leaders of industry, who were transforming the economy with profound consequences, were 'feudalized', absorbed into the aristocracy that held the reins of power.

This strange fusion of archaic and modern tendencies was also evident in the cultural life of Imperial Germany, the most vivid example being Richard Wagner, who resurrected ancient Teutonic myths and mediaeval craft culture as subjects for the most advanced artistic and musical ideas of his age. In other countries and cultures a similar search of the past for symbols of identity was evident, with results that were often quaintly anachronistic. The monumental works of Wagner, however, aroused an elemental resonance amongst audiences going far beyond aesthetic pleasure or patriotic fervour, creating rather a mystical sense of identity and mission. Referring to the overture to *Die Meistersinger*, Nietzsche wrote, 'This kind of music expresses best what I think of the Germans: they are of the day before yesterday and of the day after tomorrow. Today has not yet come.' [2]

The most familiar and enduring visual images of this period are the castles built by Wagner's patron, King Ludwig II of Bavaria, the so-called 'Mad King', which stemmed from the late 1860s. These were Herrenchiemsee, modelled on Versailles and built on an island in a lake to the east of Munich, and Neuschwanstein and Linderhof, which lay in the Alpine foothills to the south of the city. In addition, existing royal homes such as the Munich Residenz were also extensively remodelled. The style of these undertakings was essentially Rococco, though more in terms of a free interpretation than a direct copy. The interiors of these buildings brought extensive commissions for furniture craftsmen and interior designers in Munich, such as the court furnisher, Anton Possenbacher, and the master art-cabinet-maker, Franz Fortner. Of all Ludwig's projects, only Linderhof was substantially completed before his final illness and death, and in it too can be found a strange blend of ancient and modern. The Venus Grotto of the castle, with a small pool on which Ludwig was rowed in a shell-shaped boat, was based on images from the first act of Wagner's *Tannhauser*. On one level it was an astonishing caprice, a retreat into a dream-like past that never existed. Ludwig's fantasy, however, was only realizable with the aid of artificial lighting, provided by the Siemens dynamos in Bavaria's first generating plant, with bulbs in five colours enabling the mood of the grotto

The Venus Grotto, Schloss Linderhof, Bavaria 1876-7. One of 'Mad King' Ludwig's favourite retreats, it lies on a hillside above the palace and required the resources of modern technology to realize its fantasy: seven stokers firing boilers to maintain a constant temperature, lights in five colours powered by an electrical generator and stalactites made from iron rods covered in concrete.

Chandelier designed by Adolf Seder, 1872. The material is unidentified but would probably be an assembly of brass castings.

to be changed. Linderhof, and Ludwig's other castles, were certainly exceptional cases, only possible because of his position and wealth, but in a very real sense they expressed attitudes which in varying degrees, according to means, were widely manifested in homes throughout Germany.

Nowhere, it seems, did the past have such a hold over the national imagination as in Germany, embodying a sense of manifest destiny that would be revealed at some future time. Such attitudes imply a deficient sense of reality in confronting contemporary problems, which whilst not universally true, was certainly so for a significant body of reaction to the defeat of France in 1871. Many eulogized victory as a triumph of German morals and culture, a sign of their country regaining its ancient power and identity and a promise of replacing a declining France as leader of world culture. This theme of cultural mission grew more persistent in succeeding decades, yet one must remember its source was a victory achieved by superior technology and organization, by force of arms. The confusion of efficiency with morality was hardly a uniquely German characteristic, since it was also evident in contemporary justifications of imperial expansion, of the 'civilising mission' of Britain and France. It was more a difference of tone, with the new sense of German nationalism releasing a pent-up vigour, often expressed in stridently assertive terms that grated harshly abroad, but which nevertheless was a significant focus of endeavour and aspiration within Germany.

The most immediate and evident impact of unification on Germany, however, was a period of wild economic boom and speculation known as the *Gründerzeit*, the founding period, so-called from the number of companies that were founded. The enthusiasm and high expectations generated by military victory were fuelled by the large amounts of capital made available by the French payment of an indemnity of 5 million francs and

Clockface by Anton Seder, 1872. The lavish decoration, derived from Baroque forms, almost obscures the object's function. Even the clockface is so ornate it becomes difficult to read.

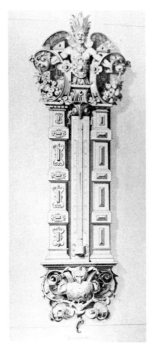

Household thermometer designed by Ferdinand Bartz, 1875. Even the smaller objects were subjected to heavy decoration, which in this case lacks any stylistic consistency or relationship to function.

Design for a doorknocker in bronze by Th. Dennerlein, 1873. Casting this conceit accurately would have created enormous technical problems, given its small scale and minute detail.

the annexation of Alsace and Lorraine with their thriving industries as part of the peace settlement. In the optimistic frenzy that resulted, economic growth, large government orders, a building boom with a demand for domestic comforts, an expanding market for luxury goods and free-spending attitudes, affected all areas of production including the applied arts. A few years later a commentator noted: '... the *Gründer* (speculators) were the princes of the day. The art industries are weighted by the parvenu like no other, he has the active need to do things the same as others, and the statue or the vase, the table-setting and the carpet, etc., should at least give the appearance of old culture and of station.' [3] Since over-decoration was often confused with status, or credit-worthiness, the ostentatious spending of the period led to an emphasis on ornate display, catered for by a rich mixture of historical forms and materials. But it was not only through such patronage that the art industries felt the influence of that

time. Commercial expansion and takeovers altered the composition of many companies, with a new emphasis on size, and an impersonal managerial organization very different to the old-established pattern of a director whose personal skill and taste were the active ingredients for success. The shift of emphasis from personal experience and intuition to a more emphatically commercial view of the art market was perhaps the most lasting legacy of the *Gründerzeit* in the sphere of applied art.

The round of feverish speculation, in which there was widespread swindling, collapsed in 1873, leading to ruin and loss for many. In the depression that ensued, domestic problems were compounded by the effect of imports from Germany's international competitors. This was particularly true for the art industries, as French producers began to reassert themselves and reclaim markets lost during and after the war. Demands for tariff protection from both industrial and agricultural interests, the so-called alliance of 'iron and rye', led ultimately to the abandonment of free-trade by the end of the decade. Parallel to the growth in protectionism came demands for the establishment of a national style in the applied arts that would symbolize Germany's new found unity and cultural identity. Linked to nationalistic feeling and the sense of cultural mission also developing at this time, it was to profoundly shape the subsequent course of both theory and practice in the applied arts in Germany.

2   The Applied Arts in the *Gründerzeit*

Due to the political fragmentation of Germany prior to unification, there was no national capital to act as a magnet for talent and establish a position of cultural dominance, as was the case in the nineteenth century with Paris and, increasingly, London. Instead, patronage was spread across state capitals and regional centres, a pattern persisting to this day, giving an enviable breadth and diversity of provision. In addition, the later start to industrialization meant traditional, regional crafts survived more widely than was the case in Britain, though under increasing pressure from mechanized production.

The political and industrial power of Britain was a model many Germans looked to in mid-century and the impact of the 1851 Great Exhibition in London provoked enormous interest. In the 1860s, the term *Kunstgewerbe*, or applied art, first came into widespread use as discussions evolved about how German industry could effectively compete in international markets. Typical of the interest developments in Britain evoked was a highly detailed study that appeared in 1866, *Die Forderung der Kunst-Industrie in England* (The Promotion of Art Industry in England), by Dr Herman Schwabe. This emphasized the establishment of a national art school and museum in South Kensington, of a chain of schools and museums in the provinces, and measures such as prizes, competitions, purchasing of plaster casts etc. believed to enhance knowledge and practical capability. The book concluded many of these measures were capable of translation to German conditions with great potential benefit.

Unification brought a new sense of urgency to such considerations. Local and particularist sentiment survived after 1871, but superimposed upon it was a desire to find a unified form of expression appropriate to the recently generated sense of national identity. A negative aspect of these efforts also became evident in xenophobic demands for the rejection of French and British influences in particular, which was widely seen to be necessary for the creation of a national style. Paradoxically, however, the call for unity produced even greater confusion than had hitherto existed, as advocates of an astonishing variety of historical and regional styles proposed their particular favourite for wider adoption. Clearly, what was recognised as desirable in theory was difficult to achieve in practice.

If competitive display was an essential feature of the new industrial capitalism which developed in the nineteenth century, the exhibitions so typical of the age were a wholly appropriate manifestation of this trait. International events enabled comparisons to be drawn, often jealously so, with the performance of other nations. Within states, however, there were also frequent exhibitions on a variety of themes to demonstrate the tastes, fashions and achievements currently of interest. One such event, organized soon after unification, and therefore an early indicator of the international standing of the new Reich was the Vienna World Exhibition of 1873. Germany's relationship with Austria was close, based on common cultural and linguistic ties, but there was also a competitive edge accentuated by recent history. However, whilst the new Germany aspired to parity with the long-established Austrian Empire, it had no city to match Vienna, the undisputed cultural Mecca of central and eastern Europe. Its cosmopolitan vitality and accessibility made it an easy and constant point of reference for many German artists, and from it, there was a continuing flow of influences and trends which profoundly influenced German art and culture, a fact often overlooked with the predominant emphasis on Parisian influence in those fields.

For the many Germans who visited Vienna in 1873 the results were chastening, according to Julius Lessing, a lecturer at the Berlin School of Architecture, who in the same year was appointed Director of that city's Museum of Applied Art. In a series of articles, later published in book form, he reviewed the exhibition as a whole and concluded that in comparison with its competitors, the German exhibits were lacking in quality, originality and a sense of identity. He was forthright in his judgements: 'What is above all necessary for us now, is the fundamental understanding of the dismal condition in which we find ourselves. Who does not see it, does not want to see it or cannot see it? We so often hear it is Germany's duty to free itself from the example of foreign countries, especially France, but since initially we still have to do so much to even approach what France and other countries are capable of, we must be happy to have examples on which we are able to raise our applied art, and there is nothing more zealously to be done than to study what is offered to us here.' [4] In his diagnosis of why this condition existed, Lessing emphasized the contemporary nature of German society, as in comments on the furniture section: 'The contrast which at present exists between the rich house-owner and the less wealthy classes who have to live in rented accommodation, is also completely impressed upon the furniture industry. Of expensive and simple furniture, which in earlier times had indeed more simple but equally as characterful forms as the expensive, there happens now to be little or in fact none. This area is left to humdrum craft means or easily prepared mass-products, which in the creation of forms have in mind nothing other than the saving of materials and labour. Creative powers are entirely applied to luxury industries, and only in this area is anything fresh and of artistic value to be noticed.' [5] Lessing obviously saw

in this a condition of decline, for which the remedy in the applied arts was defined as 'restoration'. The French Revolution was blamed for breaking the ties and continuity of tradition, and also machine-work, which had 'killed the true artistic and spiritual element in the crafts.' [6] To restore the crafts it was necessary to encourage old methods and models. If at first, new craftsmen would be bound to imitate the old, they could, with time and practice, develop original ideas in the spirit of the old. What was of most importance, he stressed, was that public and workers should be aware that 'a healthy, truly satisfying applied art could only arise from the quality of materials and the excellence of workmanship, and not surrogates and poor imitation, even when these stem from the best artists, which would eventually perish on the lies from which they arose.' [7] Although initially the impetus must come from luxury goods for the educated section of society, 'sensible and beautiful goods would be able to be produced for each level of consumption, if the owners would only have regard to the nature of the matter and not to empty appearance.' [8]

Lessing's uncompromising assessment was widely recognized as an indication of the new Germany's disadvantage in the applied arts. A determination to remedy this lay behind the organization of a domestic exhibition, intended as the first of a series to stimulate both the practical attainment of, and public interest in, a national style in the applied arts.

Die deutsche Kunst und Kunstindustrie-Ausstellung (The German Art and Art Industry Exhibition) took place at Munich in the Glaspalast between 15th July and 15th October 1876, and was organized by the *Bayerischer Kunstgewerbeverein* (Bavarian Applied Art Association). A colonnaded entrance to the exhibition was surmounted by a statue of the symbolic female figure of Germania, and passing through into the entrance-hall, visitors were confronted by a richly gilded wrought-iron gate in late Renais-

Title-page of the journal of the Bavarian Applied Art Association journal, 1877, with artistic riches being showered on its readership from a treasure-chest.

temporary work in art and applied art respectively.

The central location of the historical section was deliberate and symbolic. One of its organizers, the brass-founder, Ferdinand von Miller, wrote: 'We wish above all to confirm the merit of Germany through an historical applied arts exhibition and rescue the honour of our fathers and our fatherland. We want to prove to the whole world, what has once in Munich and in Germany been created.'[9] Its purpose was to review the achievements of Germany's past as an inspiration to contemporary endeavours. One report of the exhibition declaimed: 'With pride may we step through this portal, in order to delight in the magnificent works of olden times.'[10] Some three thousand works of all kinds were assembled, many from the treasure-rooms of states and cities of every German land, but whilst admiration for these objects was unbounded, a warning note was also sounded: 'Not only the forms, the techniques applied to the exhibited objects, but also the economic and social conditions under which they originate and show themselves in a relationship, must above all be taken into consideration, if the endeavours of our age for improvement are to be attended with success.'[11] This stress upon applied art as an expression of the age was to be a constant theme, although at the time focussing predominantly on what past style, considered in terms of its cultural connotations, was most suitable for adoption as a national style. In the historical section of the 1876 exhibition, work from the German Renaissance predominated, in the belief it most aptly reflected the contemporary German spirit.

A powerful advocate of this idea was Gottfried Semper, one of the most influential theorists of the age. Trained as an architect, he began to establish a reputation in Dresden, but was forced to flee Germany due to involvement in the 1848 Revolution. Thereafter he led an itinerant existence, staying first in

sance style on which was inscribed the slogan of *Unserer Väter Werke* (Our Fathers' Works). This central gate led to an exhibition of historical works, whilst to right and left were entrances leading to sections displaying con-

15

London during the 1851 Great Exhibition and subsequently working on the establishment of the South Kensington Museum. He later lived in Paris, Munich, Vienna and Zurich (where he stayed longest) before his death in Rome in 1879.

Semper paid considerable attention to the applied arts in his writings, which were based upon wide-ranging historical studies. Two concepts fundamental to his theories in this respect were those of 'types' and 'symbolic form'. For Semper, the concept of type was the irreducible form of an object determined by its original needs. This might be modified in other societies or periods by the nature of the materials available for production, though still retaining the fundamental type characteristics. The concept of types related primarily to functional qualities, such as the specific characteristics, for example, that determine what is a chair or a jug. In addition, however, Semper recognized that traditions and social conventions were also capable of being expressed through objects, and his concept of symbolic form encompassed anything which could be identified as intellectual or spiritual content. Only symbolic form, he argued, could make a work of art out of an object of use.

Whilst Semper's concept of type was later to be used in the 1920s as a justification for the 'machine aesthetic' of simple geometric forms, his contemporary influence was directed more towards defining an appropriate style for the age. His historical research led to an advocacy of the Renaissance, which for Semper possessed the virtues of a style combining a clear purpose with a sense of middle-class order. The basic structures of the Renaissance had a functional logic, with which decoration was combined as an integral element of the overall form, rather than a feature with an independent purpose or existence. Since it was seen as a bourgeois, rather than a courtly, aristocratic style, Semper argued it was the most appropriate for adaptation by contemporary society, a view that was widely shared.

In the organization of the applied art section at Munich there was one notable innovation. Rather than solely exhibiting products in separate categories, such as furniture, metalware and ceramics, for the first time in Germany a central feature of the exhibition was a series of rooms in which a range of objects was organized to create a unified effect, a concept of ensemble derived from France. However, although furniture structure was once again being emphasized, and the extent of upholstery was reduced from the inflated proportions fashionable around the 1850s, it was not always possible in practice to achieve the desired unity in each room. Moreover, although the Renaissance dominated the historical section, and was indeed well-represented in contemporary exhibits, there was also evident a range of other styles, from Old German and Gothic through to Rococo.

In this gamut of stylistic imitations there was obviously no evidence of a unified approach and although new techniques and high skills were sometimes apparent, no attempt was made to evolve new concepts of style from them. A comment on the highly regarded exhibit of the Eisenwerk Ilsenburg, specialists in cast-iron, is indicative of the general tendencies of the time: 'Mostly they are imitations of old implements, plates, tables, containers etc., which are modelled and moulded in true emulation of the old art-works. In all the articles one sees how well the metal and materials of the forms are chosen and what fine taste and cultivated art-sense here holds sway.' [12] Although the products were commended for the way cast-iron was used in its own right, without attempting to imitate other materials, in formal terms a strong adherence to past styles and conventional canons of taste predominated.

Amidst the confusion of stylistic claim and counter-claim, there were, however, attempts to assert other perspectives. In a detailed review of the exhibition, Oskar Mothes wrote that if the task for Germany was 'to break the French nimbus, create a new style of art and educate and win the public for the same',[13] then 1876 did little to further these ends. Too many exhibits provided reminiscences of the events of 1870-71 on objects having nothing to do with them, and there was an excess of overdecoration. Moreover, wrote Mothes, there was relatively little support from the public and press, and despite the efforts of the applied arts movement, little evidence of influence on the major trade fairs held at Leipzig. Museums were criticized, and by implication the historical exhibit at Munich, for raising expectations of *Wunderdinge* (miracle objects), so that the public 'wanted to have unalloyed beauty for little money.'[14] His main criticism of the exhibits, however, focussed on designs in which 'too little attention has been paid to the qualities of the materials concerned, to the established techniques of the production section concerned, in short to easy and inexpensive feasibility.'[15]

The solution he advocated was to improve the education system, in connection with which much of his review focused on the schools section of the exhibition. Manufacturers were quoted as complaining that young graduates from applied arts schools considered themselves artists, and were unwilling to adapt to the constraints of production for the market, or demanded such high fees that products were made more expensive. There was no doubt justification for these strictures, but Mothes failed to point out that complaints of this nature were also at the root of the attitude of wanting much for little which he had earlier criticized. Future improvement, he argued, hinged upon changes in applied art schools, emphasizing the nature of materials and techniques and developing individual freedom in students. As a model, the Royal Applied Art School in Munich under the direction of an architect, Professor Emil

Lange, was cited. Instruction there began with general preliminary studies through lectures and exercises, followed by 'special studies through practical activity in specific areas of applied art, the teaching programme based not on general class instruction, but more a specific course of instruction for each pupil prescribed by the teaching body.'[16] There were obviously problems in providing adequate resources in some institutions, however, the drawing school at Breslau being hindered by having only three teachers for 139 pupils. In contrast, the Royal Saxon Applied Art School at Dresden had 9 teachers to 52 pupils. At the latter a clear distinction was made between the education of *dessinateure* and *zeichner*. Mothes commented somewhat bitingly that the dictionary did not distinguish between them, but he supposed the former was a designer (*entwurfer*) and the latter a mere copyist.[17] Generally, however, he was of the opinion that education and applied art were far more advanced in southern Germany than in the rest of the country.

There was also a congress in connection with the Munich exhibition which considered the subject of education. Although a late alteration of dates meant that participants were fewer in number than expected, the meeting recommended that art schools be established in all industrial areas; that students should be required to submit evidence of practical ability when applying for entrance; that evening schools should be provided for working craftsmen; and that such institutions should no longer be considered preliminary schools for academies of fine art. In addition, a formal initiative was undertaken which had widespread influence. It was decided to establish applied art associations in all major cities to provide a permanent forum for artists, craftsmen and their sympathisers and supporters.[18] These were to be associated in a national body to promote applied art. The *Deutsche Kunstgewerbeverein* grew steadily and by 1886, had forty-one member associations totalling 17,352 members. [19]

For the supporters of the Renaissance style, however, the Munich exhibition was claimed as an overwhelming victory. In this, a leading figure was again Julius Lessing. After studying classical philology and archaeology, he had turned to the applied arts, influenced, above all, by the ideas of Semper. His debt was evident in a lecture given in Berlin in 1877 and subsequently published, which gives an insight into why questions of style were such a preoccupation at that time. Underlying his arguments was a belief in the constancy of eternal verities, which needed to be redefined in accordance with the needs of the age, to which was added a rejection of the notion of progress and constant innovation. A style of art, he stated, was as incapable of being invented as was a language. Art forms, like language, only have living significance as the expression of a particular view of life and particular influences, such as human well-being, climatic relationships, the material environment. These remain constant through all variations of style, as does the basic root of language despite the dialects that might emerge. It was therefore not necessary or indeed even desirable to invent a new style, but rather to consider which of those in existence most clearly epitomised the fundamental characteristics of nature, time and place. He discussed at length the qualities of various styles, antique, Gothic, Baroque amongst others, but none of these, in his view, satisfied the needs of the day. There was little doubt about his choice. 'I believe we must say on the basis of the Munich exhibition, that effectively in connection with the best forms of the Renaissance, the common way to the development of a viable German style has been found.' [20] As with his earlier argument on the restoration of the crafts, he believed in time a new impetus could emerge from what at first would be imitation, and he ended his lecture in ringing tones: 'What we claim, if we revive again the formal world of the Renaissance, if from it we wish to newly create the national German style, is more than a claim of aesthetic insight and historical judgment, it is a challenge from the whole spiritual course of the German nation, it is a summons of art, of the mighty history of recent years, a call of the Fatherland.' [21]

If the preconditions were accepted, it was a logical and appealing argument which gained many adherents. It had one weakness, however. The success claimed for the style at Munich was based essentially on the historical section, prepared by museum staff and academics, which constructed a view of history confirming the Renaissance as a golden age of German art. Even amongst those who turned to history as a reference, many doubted its suitability, and although gaining considerable public popularity it never approached the status of a broadly acceptable style, but remained one alternative amongst many.

Despite the euphoria of the Renaissance advocates, there was a sense of disappointment at the outcome of the Munich exhibition, which was compounded by widespread discomfiture at the reaction to the German pavilion at the Philadelphia World Exhibition in the USA in the same year. The selection of exhibits on display was felt to be poor, generally attributed to the inefficiency of the Imperial government officials responsible for organizing the German section, who provided too little information too late and created administrative problems over whether unsold goods from the exhibition could be admitted back into Germany duty free. At the end of 1876 it was obvious to anyone involved in the applied arts that, both at home and abroad, much needed to be done if Germany was to have a role in the commercial and cultural competition of the age.

3 Unity and Diversity

A central problem in effecting change in the applied arts was to convince a broad public that it mattered. It was widely recognized amongst those involved that achieving artistic unity did not simply depend on resolving the stylistic confusion, but also on a broader range of extra-aesthetic factors. If there was a need to inaugurate a new age of German creativity as a unifying force for the whole nation, it was not necessarily perceived to be relevant or important by all sections of the population, and indeed the possibility of achieving it was hampered by divisions in contemporary German society. The aristocracy existed in a privileged world of their own, but not necessarily in feudal isolation. Both the involvement of aristocrats in commerce and the acceptance of industrial leaders into the aristocracy suggest a degree of adaptation to modern conditions, but support for cultural reform does not seem to have loomed large in the concerns of this group. Neither was it evident at the other end of the social spectrum. Germany had the most numerous and highly-organized working-class movement in Europe, but its representatives were embattled in a struggle for fundamental rights and recognition. Although artists such as Käthe Kollwitz and Heinrich Zille were to identify with this movement and produce powerful images of the workers' condition, the debate on national culture bore little relationship to the aims or needs of organized labour as they were defined at the time.

Even in the middle classes there were divisions of interest and emphasis. In recently established industries, such as electrical technology and chemicals, and in many companies of small or medium size producing finished goods, there was bitter resentment at the power exercised by the heavy industry-agrarian alliance, which resulted in high tariff barriers and problems for exporters. Some support for cultural reform could be found amongst this group, but it was not an inevitable corollary.

Industrialization created a newly-enriched bourgeoisie who predominantly, on the surface at least, imitated the life-style and visual culture of the aristocracy. Decoration was a cypher of accumulated wealth and social aspiration that was not simply imitation, but an appropriation of social position. Moreover, status-seeking, evident in the extent of display and decorative excess, based on an assertive individualism in commerce, was hardly an appropriate basis for a unified culture.

There was, however, an older middle class tradition in Germany which also asserted itself in the years after unification. Much of the impetus for a cultural reform movement seems, in fact, to have stemmed from this source, the inheritors of the old *burger* tradition of civic and corporate responsibility and artistic patronage, of sober taste and simple forms. Their aspirations in the new state focused on prosperity and social harmony at home and a vigorous foreign policy to establish Germany's place as a major power in the world. The National Liberal movement in politics was a manifestation of this outlook, though it was a notable failure in its attempts to gain effective power. It would be a mistake, however, to view political achievement as the sole indicator of success for this element of society. Cultural unity was not considered simply as a mirror of social or political endeavours, but as a vital force in its own right, capable of supplanting politics, of going beyond political and social divisions to help create a harmonious society.

It was this emphasis on the role of applied art in society which gave the cultural debate in Germany its cutting edge and appeal, and whilst it might not have commanded universal support, the movement to create a national style did not fail for lack of endeavour, neither

Sideboard designed by Joseph Durm and executed by Fa. Himmelheber of Karlsruhe, c.1880. This elaborate piece in Renaissance style was typical of much furniture of the period, both in scale and decoration.

Great Exhibition, museums of applied art were established throughout Germany from the mid-1860s onwards, covering all the major cities, Berlin, Munich, Hamburg, Leipzig, Cologne and many others. Their collections were intended to provide sound historical examples relating to local industry, and they also offered a range of organized activities for practitioners and for the general public, such as competitions for new designs and lecture programmes. At the Berlin Applied Art Museum in the first quarter of 1887, for example, two free lecture courses were offered to the public: a series of ten on 'Furniture from Past to Present' and six on 'Development of Letter Forms'. [22]

Museum directors frequently exercised an authority extending far beyond the limits of contractual duties and played a significant role in the cultural life of Imperial Germany, as was evident in the activities of Julius Lessing referred to earlier. Following his appointment as Director of the Museum of Applied Art in Berlin in 1873, he showed tremendous energy in reorganizing the museum and its collections and, in 1881, saw the completion of a new building. He was then thirty nine years of age and his influence was at a peak. In the 1880s he became a close advisor of Crown Prince Friedrich Wilhelm and Crown Princess Victoria (the eldest daughter of Queen Victoria). The royal couple espoused liberal social and political views, and were enlightened patrons of the applied arts. In this, the Crown Princess, who was recognized as the intellectual force in the partnership, followed the example of her father, Prince Albert. Liberal supporters anticipated that when the Crown Prince succeeded to the throne a new age would be inaugurated. Lessing had widely argued that state and public bodies should accept responsibility for artistic patronage, using such means as public buildings and memorials, the artistic decoration of all public spaces and places of assembly. It was a vision he could hope to realize under the auspices of his royal

was it entirely lacking in noteworthy achievement.

There were, for example, substantial developments in establishing museums and new educational initiatives on the lines suggested by Hermann Schwabe. Following the example of the South Kensington Museum established in 1851 with profits from London's

Glassware with silver mountings designed by Nikolaus Trübner of Heidelberg for Daum Bros. of Nancy, 1893-6. These costly artefacts required high craft skills for their realization and were a cypher of social status, which less expensive industrial products frequently sought to imitate. (courtesy: Badisches Landesmuseum, Karlsruhe)

1. To promote the people's understanding of the historical development of art industry and to have an improving effect upon the formation of taste.

2. To provide authentic prototypes for the crafts.

3. The resuscitation of lost or neglected technical methods.

4. The provision of examples of modern art industry.

patrons once they occupied the throne. For Lessing and the other liberal hopefuls, however, there was to be a cruel disappointment. When the Emperor Wilhelm I died in March, 1888, it was too late for the Crown Prince. Proclaimed as Emperor Friedrich III, he was already suffering from cancer of the throat and died three months later. With the subsequent accession of Wilhelm II to the throne, a very different emphasis set in at court. Lessing's ability to influence policy at a high level declined and he concentrated henceforward more on his writing.

Under the reign of Wilhelm II, the director of the Kaiser Friedrich Museum in Berlin, Wilhelm von Bode, who entered the museum service in 1872, emerged as a figure of international repute for his work in building up the city's art collections to a scope and standard of the highest level. A close friend of the Kaiser's, he used his position to secure large-scale public and private funding for his projects. His career was crowned in 1906, when appointed General Director of all Berlin's museums.

In Hamburg, the founding-director of the Museum of Applied Art, Justus Brinckmann, similarly had a career of great length devoted to one institution. In 1866, whilst studying law, Brinckmann had visited Vienna and its museum of applied art, and published an article proposing a similar institution for Hamburg. Its purposes were to be:

However, Brinckmann was unable to get immediate support and for some years worked as a journalist and secretary to the Hamburg Chamber of Commerce. In the latter capacity, he attended the Vienna World Exhibition in 1873 to observe developments in furniture production, and his report to the Chamber confirmed Lessing's views. Brinckmann wrote: 'We may have no illusions about the applied art inferiority and technical poverty of our furniture industry in comparison with those of other great countries.' [23] The visit reinforced his earlier conviction of the need for a museum and he began work on the project with some support from patrons in Hamburg. The museum opened in rented rooms in 1874 and in 1877 was taken over by the city with Brinckmann as director. Under his guidance it became one of the most prestigious of its kind in Europe. Among his innovations was an emphasis on 'extra-artistic' factors, or the cultural context in which art is produced, which he applied to contemporary as well as historical work, in order to stress the links between art and everyday life.

The extent of the influence of museums and their staff on what was considered appropriate in applied art in the late nineteenth century, is evident from an overview of the journals on the subject published in the 1870s and 1880s, such as *Kunstgewerbeblatt* and *Kunst und Gewerbe*. The editorial staff were predominantly drawn from the museums service and the articles were overwhelmingly historical in nature. Given that dominance, it must have been difficult to conceive of an alternative to historical style as the point of emphasis in any discussion of applied art.

A further element in the primacy of museums and history in consideration of this area, is the fact that many museums also had schools of applied art attached to them, or working in close co-operation. These were often of considerable size: the Dresden school, mentioned earlier, for example, founded in 1875, expanded rapidly to produce 5-600 trainee designers annually for industry by 1889. [24] The school in the small town of Hanau, near Frankfurt, had a total of 429 male and 58 female students, the boys being mainly apprentices in local goldware and jewellery industries, the girls mostly training in art-needlework, and links with local industry were evidently close: 'The sphere of influence of the school broadened, because manufacturers recognized the great usefulness of the instruction for industry'. [25]

Evidence of curricular patterns is provided by the Düsseldorf School of Applied Art, founded in 1883, which had a tripartite division of elementary, technical and evening schools. The latter provided opportunities for part-time study by those in employment desiring to improve their qualifications. Instruction in the elementary school, entry at fourteen years, included freehand-drawing from life and flat and plaster ornaments, geometric drawing, lectures in ornamental form including colour, with required attendance of eight hours a day for one year. The technical school offered classes in:

1. Furniture, fittings and architectural drawing;

2. Decorative painting;

3. Figurative drawing and painting;

4. Ornamental and figurative modelling in clay and wax, linked to:

5. Ornamental and figurative wood-carving;

6. Embossing, engraving and chasing.

Students also had to attend classes in drawing from plaster-casts, surface-decoration design, exercises in perspective, and lectures on anatomy and style. Discreetly placed at a later stage of the course were classes in life drawing from nude models. The evening school ran similar courses from 7-9pm. [26] The division into preliminary year and then choice of professional class was widespread practice and later developed, though with a very different emphasis, as the basic principle of the influential Bauhaus system of instruction. Of contemporary significance, however, was the scale and range of training in schools such as Düsseldorf, and the relationships established with local employers. Whilst the emphasis in both education and manufacture was on historical styles of ornament and decoration and the influence of the academic tradition was strong, students also received a sound craft training, though intended to develop executant skills rather than creative originality.

The dominance of historical precedent was still clearly evident at a second major exhibition held in Munich, intended as a follow-up to that of 1876, the *Deutsch-Nationalen Kunstgewerbe-Austellung* of 1888. There were many problems in organizing this event. Originally it was to have been held in Berlin but no public support was available and attempts to raise private funds proved inadequate. Munich was due to hold an international art exhibition in 1888 and it was decided to add applied art to it, even though it meant constructing a new pavilion. The available facilities and the enthusiasm of local supporters in Munich were cited by one writer as key factors in the realization of the idea, 'and last but not least, the beer, whose producers can always be relied upon to subscribe to financial guarantees.' [27]

Perspective view and ground-plan drawing by L. Gmelin of the exhibition buildings for the German National Applied Art Exhibition of 1888 held in Munich on the banks of the River Isar.

Balcony corner in the living-room of the Landshut Collective Exhibit, Munich 1888, designed by R. Neueder, using a free interpretation of Renaissance forms.

Facade of the Würtemburg pavilion, Munich 1888 by the architectural partnership of Eisenlohe and Weigle of Stuttgart, in which Baroque influences predominated.

Left and upper right, a presentation cup and dish by the metalware firm of P. Bruckmann of Heilbronn, lower right a tea and coffee service by Ed. Foehr of Stuttgart, all dating from 1888.

Perſpektiviſche Anſicht des Ausſtellungsplatzes.

Grundrißanordnung der Ausſtellungsbauten.

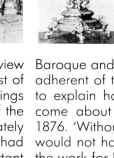

The exhibition did not give a balanced view of achievement at that time, the high cost of transport meant that rooms and furnishings were not sent from more distant parts of the country, and many areas were inadequately represented. Even those that were had museums playing an inordinately important role.

Arthur Pabst, Director of the Cologne Museum of Applied Art and editor of *Kunstgewerbeblatt* thought there was a lack of high standard exhibits and noted that Munich producers took the lion's share of space and attention. Pabst's analysis was predominantly stylistic, emphasizing the dominance of Baroque and Rococco. He was obviously an adherent of the Renaissance and concerned to explain how such a change could have come about since the apparent victory of 1876. 'Without doubt,' he concluded, 'things would not have come so far in Munich, had the work for King Ludwig II not directly given rise to, indeed required the manufacturers to adopt the Louis XIV style.'[28]

Rococco was not without its defenders, however, and its case was argued in the official account by F. Luthmer, who justified it from the point of view of both producers and consumers as giving scope for fantasy, imagination and the highest level of technique.

A saloon in Louis XVI style by M. Ballin of Munich, 1888.

The influence of Ludwig II was again mentioned, but Luthmer was in no doubt that for users no style was 'so comfortable, so adapted to the personage of mankind as this.' [29] He warned, however, that its diffusion must avoid 'shoddy and papier mâché,' and even though modestly, it should breathe the air of art.

In the same publication, however, a more fundamental note was sounded in a review of furniture at the exhibition, suggesting that contemporary trends in England and America should be paid more attention. 'It seems, however, as if there is no understanding existent for the practicality of this work and its usefulness for the essential middle-class fittings . . . The various attempts to create furnishings for the middle-class that are in good taste and not too expensive have as is well known had small success. The reasons for this were various; mostly stemming though from the false preconception that this furniture must indeed cost little, but look very expensive.' [30]

It seemed obvious to many that little had fundamentally changed since 1876. Once again, there was a dispute over styles which appeared increasingly irrelevant to the real needs of the age, and the second Munich exhibition proved in this respect to be a watershed. Historicism and the role museums played as its propagator began to be persistently questioned. There was no sudden change, but new avenues of thought and practice began to be explored.

However, this did not mean the end of the emphasis on style. Neither did the desire to define a national style prevent the inflow and influence of ideas from abroad. In this respect too, attempts to achieve artistic unity were counterpointed by a great diversity of tendencies. From France there was Impressionism. From Britain, came the ideas of Ruskin and Morris, and increasingly, of the Arts and Crafts movement, reinforcing existing belief in the crafts with the principle of joy in work. Japanese artefacts of great simplicity and artistry had a profound and stirring impact. There were the first signs in Belgium and France of what was later to emerge as *Art Nouveau*. Many others could be cited, for Europe at this time was a cultural melting pot.

The precise extent to which any or all of such influences affected consciousness or the course of events in Germany is not always easy to assess, but there were certainly greater opportunities to become acquainted with developments in other lands during the last two decades of the century. Not only exhibitions, but galleries, shops and publications provided a constant stimulus. One of the most notable institutions in this respect was the Hohenzollern-Kunstgewerbehaus in Berlin, a major gallery which had an international reputation. It was founded in 1879 by a successful businessman, Herman Hirschwald, who, enthused by an applied art exhibition in Berlin of that year, decided to devote himself wholly to applied art and open a gallery to show the best contemporary work in

Kitchen with tiles painted in Rococo style designed and executed by the Royal Porcelain Manufactory, Berlin, 1894. In such a setting the plain, functional appearance of the solid-fuel heated stove is an anachronism. (courtesy: RIBA)

Part of an exhibition of Arts and Crafts held in 1898 at the Hohenzollern-Kunstgewerbehaus, the gallery in Berlin run by Hermann Hirschwald. Amongst the exhibits were an overhead light-fitting by Otto Eckmann, a carpet by C.F.A. Voysey, metalwares by W.A. Benson, silverwares by C.R. Ashbee, a walnut bookcase by Charles Plumet and other furniture by Tony Selmersheim.

Germany. Hirschwald was evidently well-connected, for he gained the support of Julius Lessing and his co-director of the Museum of Applied Art, Professor Grunow and, above all, of the Crown Prince and Princess. The gallery soon became the centre for a constant series of exhibitions showing the best work from all countries. In 1885 Hirschwald established his own workshops, which designed and delivered the interiors of railway coaches for the Austrian Emperor and the King of Italy amongst many other commissions, and he was soon accepted as an authority on the applied arts, consulted by government bodies, travelling widely on official commissions and buying the best work available wherever it could be found. In 1898, for example, in an exhibition of Arts and Crafts, which included work from Germany, France and Belgium, could be found carpets by C.F.A. Voysey, electric lamps by W.A. Benson, and copper and silver ornaments by C.R. Ashbee.

Hirschwald was also very active in trying to promote the economic and commercial interests of applied art producers. He was a prime mover in the establishment of a new body to represent their interests, the

Fachverband für die wirtschaftlichen Interesse des Kunstgewerbes, (Trade Association for the Economic Interests of Applied Art) founded in 1892, acting for many years as secretary, and through lectures and contributions to its journal, helping to press its claims in an attempt to increase public awareness and patronage.

From all the numerous developments and influences of the 1880s, a powerful, common thread emerged by the end of the decade in a new attitude to nature, seeing in it the original fountainhead of inspiration and form from which new concepts could be developed, particularly as a source of ornament as an alternative to historical precedent. By the end of the decade it had gathered considerable momentum.

In 1888 an influential study by Ferdinand Moser appeared: *Ornamentale Pflanzenstudien auf dem Gebiet der Heimischen Flora* (Ornamental Plant Studies from the Sphere of Native Flora), and his ideas were rapidly

Designs for electrical
light-holders of various
types by Richard Guhr of
Dresden, 1892, which
illustrate the transition in
decoration from
historical to natural forms
begun in the 1880s.
(courtesy: RIBA)

ledge of Natural Forms in their Relation to
Applied Art), based on Meurer's work and
ideas. This stressed possibilities of evolving
stylized forms in two-and three-dimensions
from studies of nature and their application to
artefacts, textiles and buildings.

In 1890 the Prussian Ministry of Education
provided funds for Meurer to establish a
course in Rome on 'Ornamental Plant Studies',
to educate teachers in Prussian craft and
applied art schools in his concepts and
methods. Subsequently, the Prussian Ministry
of Commerce took over responsibility for
these institutions but continued to provide
scholarships for staff to study in Rome.

The impact of Meurer's ideas, in particular,
was enormous and was to fundamentally
influence the nature of applied art education
in Germany for many years. In 1904, at the
sixteenth conference of the Association of
German Applied Art Teachers in Cologne,
the main event was a lecture entitled 'The
Nature and Aim of Plant Drawing according
to Meurer'. A report on the event commented,
'I can think, however, of no applied art school
that, without the Meurer course of study at its
innermost core, is capable of sufficing for
modern requirements.' A review of one of
Meurer's books in 1909 confirmed this
estimate, remarking that he had taught the
present generation to study from nature and
not 'Our Fathers' Works', concluding:
'Meurer has been in any case one of the best
and earliest pioneers of the modern applied
art movement.' [31]

In addition to influencing education and
concepts of form, the emphasis on nature had
a wider impact. Linked to nationalist and
regional sentiment, it was a powerful force in
movements to preserve and protect the traditional, rural environment and culture, and on
another plane, was an important preparatory
stage in the evolution of *Jugendstil*, the
German variant of *Art Nouveau*.

The possibilities of establishing any new
style on a broad base were hampered, how-

taken up in applied art schools. In the follow-
ing year, 1889, Professor Moritz Meurer, a
Berlin teacher of ornamental studies pub-
lished a pamphlet *Das Studium der Natur-
formen an Kunstgewerblichen Schulen* (The
Study of Natural Forms at Applied Art
Schools), exploring the consequences for
curricula. Exhibitions on this theme were also
staged: in 1891 the Dresden Museum of
Applied Art presented *Die Anwendung der
Naturformen in der dekorativen Kunst* (The
Application of Natural Forms in Decorative
Art), and Berlin saw an *Ausstellung von
Studien zur Forderung der Kenntnis der Natur-
formen in ihrer Beziehung zum Kunstgewerbe*
(Exhibition of Studies for Promoting Know-

This 'wrought-iron, extremely elegantly equipped enamel stove', as the advertisement describes it, was manufactured in Darmstadt by the firm of Roeder Bros and was intended to function as a status-symbol, judging by the extent of decoration, as well as a cooking appliance. (courtesy: RIBA)

In 1891, the German Association for Public Health Care and the Association for the Promotion of Workers' Welfare held a competition for an oven design which could be used as cooker/heater in winter and cooker only in summer. The winning design by the Kaiserslautern Ironworks used an ingenious mechanism to divert heat in summer. Even on this 'workers' stove', however, decoration was considered appropriate and, given the ease with which it could be moulded in cast-iron, it could be done cheaply. (courtesy RIBA)

ever, by the nature of commercial competition in the market for consumer goods, which was rapidly growing and in which, above all, it was necessary to have a product that was different. Technology and economics combined to facilitate this demand. In processes such as moulding, casting and repetitive machine work, the additional work and cost of more complex forms, in terms of design, moulding and patterns, was minimal, as a proportion of the total production costs, whilst giving each item the appearance, at least, of more expensive materials and intricate detail. This was generally thought more desirable for purchasers who, of course, would be willing to pay a higher price. Product forms therefore represented the whole gamut of prevailing aesthetic preferences, indeed added to them with some highly bizarre combinations, and so proliferated the existing confusion on a massive scale. There existed a plethora of new forms, the functional imagery of machines and apparatus, but generally these were either ignored as having no aesthetic value, or given a decorative cladding to bring them within the orbit of acceptable taste.

There were the first signs, however, of a new attitude to mechanization. Curiously, some historians have identified a statement by Julius Lessing in 1887 as a portent of change, in which he declared: 'Yes, we must indeed recognize that art-and decorative-form disseminated from factories, as little as it is contributing upwards to the real development of art, is yet the first bridge over which artistic feeling crosses to the shelters of the poor.' [32] It was better to have a cheap machine-produced tapestry on the wall, he said, even if devoid of real artistic quality, than nothing. Lessing's grudging recognition of mechanization as the first, if debased, stage in elevating the poor to a state of artistic grace was more a confirmation of existing attitudes to mechanization than evidence of fundamental change. In fact, a clearer indication of his views was given in an article

published in November 1888 issue of the *Deutscher Rundschau,* in which Lessing reiterated his arguments in favour of craft work, asserting that artistic possibility only existed in individual work, and that a true blossoming of applied art would only be possible with the victory of the crafts over stereotyped factory products. In the following year this view was sharply challenged by Georg Bötticher, who felt Lessing's view of the machine rejected changes set in motion fifty years earlier. Mechanization had and would continue to replace the crafts, wrote Bötticher: 'Against that, whoever is able to preach the dogma: the crafts must and will return, deludes themselves and others with unfulfillable hopes.' What he called 'creative draughtsmen' must understand and design for machines just as craftsmen understand their tools. 'Machine work in our age is no longer synonymous with cheap wares: already it is creating works in which an artistic value must be recognized and in this it will come to ever greater perfection. The many mechanical means of reproduction now available to our draughtsmen are not damaging, but are only a further development and enrichment of techniques ...'. Bötticher ended with a plea not to oppose machines, but to find appropriate means of expression for them. 'If this happens — and why should it not happen — then through the enormous distribution of mechanically produced applied art articles of use, at least as much will be done to truly raise the applied art and artistic sensitivities of the nation, as with the state-assistance to promote applied art individual achievement suggested and demanded by Lessing.' [33] At that time, however, Bötticher's views were only a straw in the wind.

The gulf that existed in late nineteenth century Germany between progress in technical development and the search for an appropriate visual style was evident in many industries and product categories, though it could be manifested in different ways and certainly did not have a uniform effect. In the furniture industry, for example, there were new materials available such as cast-iron and papier mâché, but the traditional material, wood, remained overwhelmingly popular. Until the nineteenth century, production was small-scale, craft-based, and dominated by a small number of high-quality producers dependent upon a close-relationship with a

social elite who dictated taste. However, the scale of manufacture, the relationship of the industry to its market, and above all, the effect of mechanization, brought thoroughgoing changes. The problems of furniture craftsmen, indeed those in many traditional occupations were acute. The situation described by Gerhardt Masur in Berlin was typical of many German cities. 'Adolf Damaschke, later one of Germany's leading social reformers, has given us a moving description of his carpenter father's hopeless struggle with the mechanized furniture industry which had the advantage of credit and banking facilities not available to craftsmen. "How often, on Fridays and Saturdays, would my mother scurry down to the pawnshop to hock some precious heirloom in order to have money for the week's wages." Eventually the elder Damaschke capitulated to the all-powerful competition and contented himself with working as a repair man.' [34] Loss of skill and status often led to a bitter sense of grievance.

With the growth of middle-class wealth and increased production to meet its demands, the market relationship became impersonal and canons of taste were fragmented. Draughtsmen often had little practical experience, their competence focusing more on drawing and historical styles, so that stylistic effect became emphasized more than utilitarian purpose. An example is a sideboard believed to have been made in Dresden in the 1890s, part of a complete room furnishing in Renaissance style, of German and Hungarian oak, birch and maple, that was carved, stained, coloured, veneered and inlaid. The scale and complexity of the decorative forms and the mixture of stylistic elements leaves the function of the piece unclear. The overwhelming impression is of a composition by a *Musterzeichner*, a pattern-drawer, trained in architectural detail without concern for use or content. It was essentially a demonstration of rich materials, of decorative skill, and, ultimately, of wealth through possession. However, even though historical styles were widely used, these too were modified by the use of new mechanized forms of sawing, planing, drilling, turning, milling and veneering. The basic structures tended to become box-shaped, embellished with forms that could be repetitively produced, tending therefore to simpler geometric shapes in more uniform patterns than allowed by the evolutionary and personal possibilities of hand work.

In the production of metalwares the market relationship and mechanization similarly altered the structure of the industry, but techniques of moulding, stamping and pressing, the use of substitute alloys for pure metals, and above all the possibilities of plating by mechanical or electrolytic means, led to an emphasis on the simulation of precious metals and fine craftsmanship. It became possible to produce copies of past works which could sometimes be highly convincing, and museum collections not only provided a source of models but sometimes offered copies for sale. In 1907 the Berlin Museum of Arts and Crafts offered expensive copies of twenty seven pieces from the municipal silver treasury of Luneburg and seven other items. They were available in silver or copper and were 'made with the greatest attention to details mainly by galvano-plastic techniques and finished by hand in the workshops of the court goldsmith D. Vollgold & Sohn and Sy & Wagner . . .' [35]. Further down the market, the traditional skills of metalsmiths were not even applied to finished products, where these were wholly manufactured by industrial means, and by the 1880s an astonishing variety of such manufactured metal products were available.

In the public domain, the gulf between technological and aesthetic concepts was most strikingly apparent in the railway system. Its role in the victory of 1871, as noted earlier, was significant, despite problems caused by incompatible stock and equipment drawn from numerous private and state lines. After unification, railways remained the responsibility of federal states, and Prussia introduced a policy of nationalizing and integrating its network. In the mid 1880s, the introduction of standardized designs for locomotives and rolling stock commenced, often with interchangeable elements and components between different types. An underlying consideration was to ensure maximum efficiency and repairability in war, though there were also very considerable economic benefits in peacetime working. The result was an impressive level of technical efficiency, the so-called

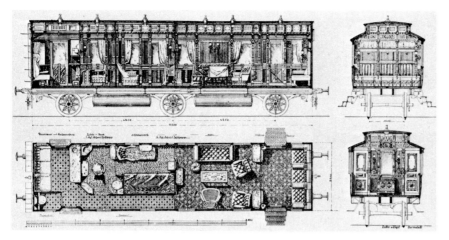

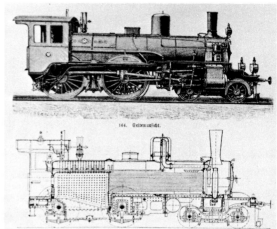

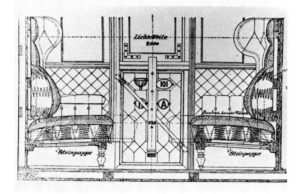

Plan, elevation and cross-section drawings of a railway saloon-car designed by architect P. Koch of Bingen in 1892.

This 4-4-0 passenger locomotive of Prussian State Railways was in widespread use in the first decade of the present century.

Cross-section of a Prussian State Railways first-class carriage c.1885. The contribution of interior coiled-springs to the comfort and plump appearance of nineteenth century furniture is here apparent.

Water-crane in cast-iron for Prussian State Railways, c.1890. These stood at the end of station platforms, the arm swinging over to fill locomotive water-tanks during station halts.

'Prussian Standards' setting the pattern for other European systems.

The locomotives built by Prussian State Railways under this programme were highly efficient machines but their design sometimes showed little attention to their overall effect as a visual form. Boilers were generally set on a high frame, giving easy access to working-parts, often with a clutter of pipes, valves and parts on the outside casing also for easy servicing. However, although considerations of safety and the functional demands of service and maintenance produced rolling-stock exteriors free of superfluous decorative encrustation, carriage interiors, buildings and static equipment were not so limited. A Prussian first-class railway carriage compart-

ment of the 1880s had an extent of padding, metal mouldings and turned wood that not only ensured the comfort of occupants but was also an indicator of social status. That was relatively rational, however, compared to the decorative mouldings adorning the cast-iron water-cranes used to fill locomotive tanks, which stood as mute testimony to cultural aspirations at the end of station platforms.

Even the most dramatic technical break-through could be subjected to similar treatment. The invention of a method of mass-producing tubular steel by the Mannesmann company in 1885 was hailed as 'a revolution within iron technology'. Previously tubes were produced by wrapping strip-steel sheet

A range of demonstration pieces by artist/smiths produced in 1891 to explore the artistic possibilities of Mannesmann tubular steel, which totally ignored the unique structural and functional properties of the material.

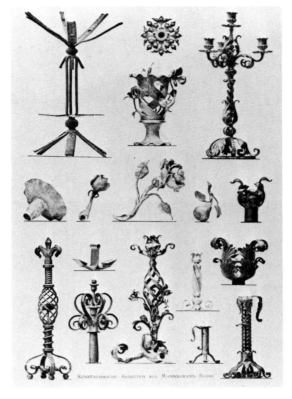

Examples used in an article published in 1891 in *Deutsche Bauzeitung* to illustrate the constructional possibilities of Mannesmann seamless tubular steel.

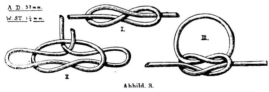

around a former and brazing the seam, a lengthy and expensive process vulnerable to error. In the new process, two rollers pulled a glowing billet of steel over a torpedo-shaped mandrel, producing high-quality seamless tube at greatly reduced cost. Such tube played no small part in the development of the bicycle as an inexpensive form of mass-transport. In an article in an architectural journal, a Mannesmann employee, W. Schleuning, explored its properties: 'The aesthetic of a material,' he wrote, 'will in itself always remain constant, and the art produced from it must now as previously remain in its predetermined, adequately broad limits, unaffected by stylistic epochs or nationality or the mood of artists. No force, no unnaturalness may be imposed on the applied art product, without it being excluded from claiming the designation of art work.' [36] Therefore the task of applied artists was to realize inherent material properties, which were demonstrated by illustrations of tubular steel bent into a variety of knotted forms. Schleuning asserted it would not be long before furniture and objects of everyday use, and he specifically mentioned the 'Vienna Chair', would be produced in tubular form to overcome the disadvantages of timber (a prophecy fulfilled in the 1920s by the cantilever chairs designed by Mart Stam and Marcel Breuer). Pride of place, and a goodly proportion of space in his article was given, however, to a series of experiments by 'academically trained artists', demonstrating the artistic possibilities of tubular steel, which were exhibited in Mannesmann's Berlin salesrooms. The results were certainly inventive, but seemed to contradict Schleuning's argument by making the material conform to contemporary interest in the ornamental properties of natural forms, rather than probe its innate structure for a new aesthetic or new functional forms. Art and technology generally remained separate areas of concept and experience at this time, and though the twain might occasionally meet, it was usually on the basis of mutual incomprehension rather than fruitful synthesis.

If, for public bodies and private individuals alike, art in everyday life was widely synonymous with decorative embellishment, by around 1890, dissatisfaction with prevailing attitudes was rife. Comment was not limited to the applied arts, however, but was part of a bitter critique of the fundamental nature of contemporary civilization, and industrialization in particular, that came to permeate wide areas of German cultural thought, giving rise to a mystical nationalism as powerfully emotive as it was frequently obscure.

4 Cultural Pessimism and the Germanic Ideology

Throughout the nineteenth century, many prominent German thinkers sought to comprehend and explain the ravelled pattern of dissolution and change which challenged traditional beliefs and ethical certainties. What is of particular relevance here is the distinctive place assigned to art in the thought of some, which was to significantly affect artists' own perception of their importance and role from the late nineteenth century onwards.

Of fundamental importance in this process were the ideas of Arthur Schopenhauer. Although he died in 1860, his work, which had been comparatively neglected in his lifetime, enjoyed a great resurgence and became hugely influential by the 1880s. In contrast to most philosophers, Schopenhauer's view of life was unredeemably pessimistic. The world as we know it, and man as part of it, presented for him a pattern of fleeting change that can be perceived but not controlled or fundamentally altered, and is utterly indifferent to moral imperatives. Knowledge cannot increase understanding and indeed can only compound man's helplessness. The only resolution of this impotent wretchedness, and here there are parallels with Eastern mythical thought, was through a cathartic transformation of consciousness to a condition liberated from desire and the bewildering confusion of the 'objective' world. This is the realm of the Platonic absolute, of eternal forms and unchanging values underlying the transience of life, the true source of understanding and inspiration for saints and artists. It was the raising of the latter to a status of comparability with seers and visionaries that was such a remarkable feature of Schopenhauer's thought. For him, each reflected a consciousness of themselves, and therefore the world, that gave metaphysical significance and ethical value to a meaningless existence. Whereas the former provides reflections in the abstract form of language on eternal verities, the perception and language of aesthetics provides concrete images, the 'thing in itself', which in its completeness embodies the essence of higher reality.

His highest esteem was reserved for painting and sculpture since architecture and the applied arts required a compromise with scientific knowledge and the concerns of the everyday world, but even though tainted in this way, they could still play a part. By rejecting all attempts to imitate the external forms of nature and instead seeking to express the essence of a structure, each part could perform its function, revealing what it is and no more. In this respect, Schopenhauer's ideas had a formative influence on the evolution of functionalist aesthetic concepts in the mid-nineteenth century, for example, in the work of architectural theorists such as Friedrich Schilling and Carl Bötticher. [37] The power of such art, at all levels according to Schopenhauer, is not simply to communicate concepts but to arouse and generate comprehension in recipients, to act as a vital agent in transforming human consciousness. Seen in this perspective, art was given a preeminence by Schopenhauer far removed from the eighteenth century concept of the subservient artisan providing decorative luxuries, that still persisted in his own time. Instead, from the depths of pessimism, artists became the great redeemers, creating a sense of affirmation and perfection from pain and disillusion.

Although influenced to a considerable degree by Schopenhauer, with Friedrich Nietzsche came a profound change of emphasis. He too shared the pessimistic view of the world. 'Towards the end of his conscious life Nietzsche was convinced that the culture of Europe was doomed; that an eclipse of all traditional values was at hand, and that European man, this pampered child of the optimistically rational eighteenth century, would needs go astray in a wilderness without path or guidance.' [38] God, for Nietzsche, was dead and the abyss of meaningless life presented in the absence of a deity could only be filled, not by a retreat into a mysticism that rejected the world, but by the Will to Power, by man confronting the world as it is and overcoming himself, Man becoming Superman.

Not only was Nietzsche's philosophy influential, but also his style and methodology. He passionately expounded an attitude to life that combined scholarship and myth, was full of inconsistencies, abounded in value-laden judgments and completely ignored academic aspirations to impartiality and objectivity. The path he trod in this respect soon became well-beaten, often by figures he would have utterly rejected as the sense of cultural loss became more strident and ferocious.

This new turn in the reaction against modernity has been designated the 'Germanic Ideology' by Fritz Stern: '. . . the elements of their cultural thought . . .constituted an ideology, at once an indictment, a program, and a mystique. This ideology I call "Germanic" because its principal goals were the revival of a mythical "Deutschtum" and the creation of political institutions that would embody and preserve this peculiar character of the Germans. All their works were suffused by this mixture of cultural despair and mystic nationalism that was radically different from the untroubled nationalism of their contemporaries.' [39]

The man who crystallized the new tendency was Paul de Lagarde, in a book entitled *Deutsche Schriften* (German Letters) published in 1886. In this work, every aspect of modernity, parliamentarism, liberalism, secularism, capitalism, amongst others, were subjected to the lash of Lagarde's emotional, hate-filled vituperation. The Jews allied to the Liberals were depicted as agents of destruction in a sinister conspiracy to subvert the German nation. Their extermination, in terms acutely foreshadowing the reality of Hitler's rule, was a precondition for the reassertion of the true *Deutschtum,* the eternal values of German culture. In essence, Lagarde created a powerful myth of simplicity, natural virtue, dynamic energy and community under heroic leadership, which embodied the nature and aspirations of the Volk and would lead them to a new age of greatness. Racism, nationalism and imperialism were instruments of purification, having little to do with conventional politics, which Lagarde contemptuously rejected.

In 1891, a seminal work appeared which elaborated the consequences for art of the Germanic ideology. In *Rembrandt als Erzieher* (Rembrandt as Educator) by Julius Langbehn, art was the antithesis of prevailing scientific and materialist trends, the only true synthesizing expression of German values, to which political and educational policy should be subservient: in short, art was to achieve the regeneration earlier advocated by Lagarde.

According to Langbehn, the prime German characteristic and the root of all artistic creativity was individuality, but it was invalid if self-interested, rather it must serve the German nation. This characteristic, a product of local identity and sense of place, was contrasted with the rootlessness of modern urban culture and had to be reasserted: 'The true artist can never be local enough.' [40] It was to small towns, therefore, that Langbehn looked as focal points for development. 'Capability rather than knowledge should motivate these towns; their powers should be dedicated to the muses rather than museums; they should relate to art education rather than art consumption.' [41] Museums had value, but only if serving art and creativity in the local context, rather than a self-referential ideal of historical scholarship.

A central concern for Langbehn was style:

'The great question of the day, indeed of the century in the realm of art is: how do we attain a new style?' [42] Only by awakening the true German spirit could it be achieved, and he specifically rejected the unthinking adoption of historical forms. 'Style is no dress that one can take on or off, it is a piece of the heart of the people themselves. Style can only develop from the deepest, most inner kernel of the personality of the people ...' [43] True style would link the conscious and unconscious nature and aspirations of the people in an 'organic' rather than a 'mechanical' manner. To rediscover the true nature of the people, however, it was necessary to return to their source, to the land and to the peasant. Education must grow from this soil, from inner nature and revitalized traditions; it must unify, looking to prophets rather than professors. However, a balance must be maintained, he asserted. Art must seek a contemporary German style, looking to the past not in terms of *Unserer Väter Werke* (our fathers' works) but of *Unserer Väter Gesinnung* (our fathers' convictions). 'The real Renaissance will prevail thus; following the spirit not the letter of ancient art; and it will thereby be itself creative.' [44]

On the subject of the applied arts, they displayed: 'much triviality and little inspiration.' [45] In the Introduction to the book, Langbehn wrote: 'The present day applied art has, through its stylistic chase, probed all ages and peoples and despite, or indeed perhaps because of this, has not achieved its own style.' [46] The eyes of the public needed opening to value spiritual rather than material qualities, and applied art stood far removed from the native spirit that was its only possibility of renewal. 'Here, as always, the people should not attempt to come nearer to the cultivated, but much rather the cultivated to the people. That which the English call "comfort" is the naturally given point of departure for all sound endeavours in this aspect; from it style should primarily develop

and not the other way round as currently practiced. If the highest convenience and the highest beauty coincide in an object of use, so it is perfect in terms of applied art.' In the final sentence Langbehn advocated a fusion of utilitarian and aesthetic considerations as an ideal in applied art, emphasizing the external demands and constraints on the former. 'Art grows from the inside to the outside, applied art from the outside to the inside. As soon as one interchanges this double-sided standpoint, art will, as in present-day architecture, become a mannerism and the applied arts, as in present predominant application, will become a pure luxury trade.' [47]

To prevent this, applied art too must return to its source, for firm guidelines and criteria. 'Applied art must not, as it now exclusively is, be a hothouse plant, it should grow in the open air, or better still, wild. Economy in the application of decorative forms must be its first rule; not voluptuousness as now predominates; in restraint above all is the master revealed.' Self-conscious artistry is derided. Indeed, Langbehn stated, 'Construction is art.' [48]

Although not developed in great detail, there are a number of key points in Langbehn's discussion of applied art that were later to be widely elaborated: the reconciliation of utility and beauty; the satisfaction of everyday needs and aspirations rather than a limited concentration on decorative luxury products; simplicity and construction as the fundamental constituents of form; and an emphasis on artefacts as vital elements in a general cultural renewal. However, this advocacy was set in the context of an ideology that prefigured, and by creating a mental climate and justification must also have encouraged, the evolution of a brutal authoritarian regime. Langbehn's racism is evident: the Jews were characterized as rootless and cosmopolitan, therefore lacking in individuality and thus any creative capacity. All people of foreign blood, he proposed, should be deprived of German citizenship to purify the race. Above all, he argued, German individuality must be defended, which is turned into a justification of war: 'The nation of poets and thinkers *(Dichter und Denker)* has changed to a nation of warriors and artists *(Krieger und Kunstler)*.[49] He euloguzed 'War and Art' as a Greek, a German, an Aryan virtue, linking this to aspirations for world hegemony. 'A nation which concentrates upon itself, will also by this means automatically have mastery over others; Greece has proved it, Germany will hopefully prove it.'[50]

The realization of these aims could not succeed by means of normal political processes. Instead, said Langbehn, to inaugurate the new age of art as politics, Germany needed a 'secret Emperor', who would arise from the people. 'His own individuality must stem from the individuality of his people, mirror it in himself, cover himself with it.'[51] This pseudo-Messianic figure would be the embodiment of the German people, be their voice, think what they think, and lead, inspire and educate the nation.

Thus from cultural despair was fabricated a contemporary myth of elemental appeal. In rational terms it was deeply flawed, but precisely because it emphatically rejected rationalism and appealed to raw emotions, Langbehn's heady brew had a tremendous influence. It gave a damning critique of modernity; it asserted a sense of pride in German's past and faith in its future; its emphasis throughout was moral and, above all, it promised salvation. In fact, Langbehn's tone and impact was that of an evangelical revivalist. His message was not unique and no single movement developed out of his writings, but he crystallized a broad spectrum of discontent and gave it a focus and a sense of mission. His own political views were very obvious, but he also articulated ideas that were applicable to many political viewpoints. The reaction against cities and the desire to develop a culture closer to the soil, for example, was variously adapted across the political spectrum. Indeed, a common fact linking many of the disparate movements that sprang up in Germany in the 1890s, was antimodernism and an emphasis on art as an instrument of moral renewal.

5 New Initiatives in Cultural Reform

In juxtaposing the names of Schopenhauer and Nietzsche with the likes of Lagarde and Langbehn, there is a danger of imputing that the concepts and arguments of the former prepared the ground for the Germanic ideology. This would be unjust, for although certain of their ideas were adopted, it was often in a distorted form, applied to a concept wholly alien to their intent. The Germanic ideology that crystallized during the 1880s in fact drew on a wide range of sources, not all of them German, but although its basic tenets can be found in other countries, nowhere did they assume such importance as in Germany. In one sense it can be seen as part of a conservative reaction to the whole trend of nineteenth century civilization, equating liberal democracy and the ideas of liberty, equality and social improvement with weakness and decline. Against that negative reaction was set a powerful sense of nationalism; a concept of realizing individuality through service to the authoritarian state; a concept of the binding force of the *volk* (a term difficult to translate and meaning a people, but with emotive overtones of a racial community); and a belief in a leader embodying the spirit of a *volk,* which was sometimes equated with a parallel concept of the artist. Whilst reactionary in its attitude to the modern condition, however, it also possessed a revolutionary dynamic. Although looking to a highly idealized past, it was not directed towards a simple restoration but rather a recreation of society in which the irreversible features of modernity, science, technology and commerce, would be subordinated to the true spirit of *Deutschtum,* a quintessential Germanness.

Such ideas had wide currency in the middle classes of Germany in the late nineteenth century, and although *völkish* beliefs could degenerate into xenophobic imperialism and racism, this extremism was not an inevitable corollary. In a more muted form, many of these ideas in fact provided the motive force of a wide-ranging set of initiatives for cultural reform, in which applied art and design came to play a decisive role. These initiatives manifested themselves in a variety of forms, institutions, organizations and publications.

If art in all its forms was to play a greater part in national life, then the people had to be educated to be more understanding and receptive towards it. In this respect, museums began to play a more active and outgoing role. Typical of a new generation of museum directors was Alfred Lichtwark, Director of the Hamburg Kunsthalle. A major concern of his was the creation of a climate of public opinion in which the gulf between artist and public could be replaced by a unity of understanding. 'We have in Germany thought almost exclusively of the education of art producers . . . But our production beats the air, as long as in our own land the purchaser lacks an independent taste.' [52] The remedy for this was education. In Germany, argued Lichtwark, cultivation was considered synonymous with knowledge, and education with instruction. This confusion had led to a loss of identity and a reliance on other culture's forms and standards. To counter this, it was necessary to reassert a sense of indigenous tradition and the ability to form self-reliant judgments. What was widely evident in the sphere of music, he asserted, had to be developed in the visual arts. The task was above all educational, 'directed to the cultivation of the eyes and therefore of taste.' [53] To achieve this in schools it was necessary to move from instruction in art history, from facts which are soon forgotten, to a practical approach of seeing, enjoying and forming judgments, capacities which would last a lifetime. In 1887, courses were introduced at the Kunsthalle for serving teachers to develop these new techniques, using the museum's resources.

An educational methodology of this kind was intended to lay the foundations for a public seriously receptive to and capable of delighting in art, summed up in Lichtwark's concept of the dilettante. His theory in this respect was an ideal of aesthetic sensitivity, a layman who through contact with practitioners would become an enlightened judge, patron and promoter of art, who would ' . . . observe and diligently care for all potential, the development of which promises to increase the reserve of unique national powers.' [54] The role of the dilettante, moreover, was not simply directed to the fine arts. 'Our generation no longer recognizes a division between art and "applied art". A book cover, an embroidery can equally well contain art as a picture.' [55]

Equally as important was the role of women in forming an educated public. 'For all preferences which women today adopt, will be imbibed by coming generations with their mother's milk.' [56] The practical needs of housewives was also a benchmark for judging the effectiveness of products and their useability. In an article from 1897, he gave a series of examples, of Gothic tables at which if a seated guest made an unconsidered movement, they risked wounding their shins. Or high, wood-carved chimney pieces that were impossible to clean adequately and required a safety-ladder to reach. *Sachlichkeit*, or simple, practical fittings, easy to maintain and pleasing to the eye, were what the housewife needed, he argued, not over-decorated exhibition pieces.

Lichtwark also campaigned vigorously for folk art and regional traditions, believing the varying conditions and requirements of different parts of Germany needed to be taken into account, with local types providing a basis for the evolution of practical and aesthetic contemporary models.

His advocacy of such ideas later broad-

ened into leadership of a more comprehensive initiative, the Art Education Movement, to the first conference of which in 1901 he gave a closing address in terms very reminiscent of Langbehn: 'The demand for artistic education does not appear in isolation; from its first hour it was inextricably connected with the contemporaneous, more clearly formulated call of the mid-eighties for a moral renovation of our life. The two fields are inseparable . . . For too long we have lived essentially for intellect. It is high time now for the moral-religious and artistic forces to reach their full development.' [57]

When the Kaiser Wilhelm Museum in Krefeld was founded in 1897 to forge links with local industry, one of Justus Brinkmann's assistants from Hamburg, Friedrich Deneken, was appointed Director, and his vigorous approach to his duties achieved widespread attention. Of the museum in 1898, *The Studio* reported: 'The inauguration was celebrated by an exhibition of paintings, sculpture, china and pottery . . . In the ceramic section the museum purchased works from the Berlin manufactory, from the royal manufactory of Copenhagen, and from that of Bing and Grondahl in the same town. Also pottery by de Morgan, Schmuz-Baudiss, T.F. Willumson (Copenhagen), Bigot, Dalpayrat and Dammouse, in addition to some fine specimens of glassware by Emil Gallé.' [58] This collection represented a cross-section of some of the best contemporary work on an international scale. A German visitor commented: 'With such an exhibition Dr Deneken makes manifest his complete comprehension of the task of directing the museum presented to him. For besides the cognizance of historical monuments of art, the understanding, the familiarization of the art of our time, must be fostered by exemplary works.' [59]

Deneken sought to revive regional crafts and traditions in Krefeld not only by the quality of the objects collected, but also by inviting leading artists to work with local firms and by actively using the museum, its facilities, exhibitions and collections as an artistic stimulus. Many of these endeavours were practical in nature, but there were also others of more general application, such as exhibitions on art in schools and another on colour '. . . illustrating the application of colour to all works of art, as well as its theory in nature.' [60]

Deneken's purpose was essentially conservative, an attempt to re-invigorate traditional values and give them contemporary relevance, and to promote a sense of regional and national identity. To achieve these ends he saw no contradiction in using a range of reformist ideas, including *Jugendstil,* the garden-city movement and dress-reform for women. His aim was to make the museum an agency for uniting art with local industry and social life, an instrument for revitalizing German culture and society.

The theme of cultural unity as a mirror of social unity was also evident at the *III allgemeine deutsche Kunstgewerbetag* (Third general German Applied Arts Conference) of the *Kunstgewerbeverein* held in Berlin in the summer of 1896. The key address was by Julius Lessing on the subject of 'The Place of Art and Applied Art in Public Life', and it indicated the extension of his ideas in this period.

Craft firms, he argued, had originated in the separation of applied art from high art, but it was necessary for the two to draw together again, indeed the expression 'applied art' should perhaps disappear and be replaced by 'art', which should be expressed in all forms. This was not simply a question of terminology, however, but also of practice. He advocated the replacement of formal richness by formal simplicity as a common practice, since in the provision of highly decorative goods for the luxury market there was evident 'not an abuse of applied art but a social evil'. Visual differentiation of wealth and status was socially divisive and instead, the furnishings and clothing of artisans should

not be different from the higher classes. In this respect, he expressed regret that cheap room furnishings designed for a competition sponsored by Berlin City Council had been bought not by artisans but by middle and higher officials. Simplicity was therefore advocated as a symbol of social unity and he emphasized 'objects must stand in the organic context of their purpose and not be handed over to craftsmen in the final stages.' To effect improvement, government and private bodies, indeed the whole public, needed to co-operate in promoting art. Lessing concluded: 'The true art, however, is not to be sought in monumental buildings, but in the appropriate artistic treatment of the smallest detail. In this sense the state has more to receive from art than art from the state. For art is a state sustaining moral power.' [61] He was accorded long and enthusiastic applause.

In his call for unity, Lessing noted that what was missing was the central ground of an ideal standpoint. However, the reasons for the absence of such agreement in society, or the economic and social reasons for artisans not wishing to purchase simple furniture, were unexplored. In this respect there was a contradiction in the movement for cultural reform as a whole, which by subordinating social considerations to an ideal of aesthetic unity, ignored the real social divisions then existing in Germany.

One of the most important agencies for disseminating ideas of cultural reform and a profound influence in moulding middle-class opinion, was the journal *Kunstwart,* founded in 1887 by the writer and poet, Ferdinand Avenarius. Its coverage included frequent articles on the visual arts. However, Avenarius was not content simply to write about art, but in the spirit of the time, wanted to participate more directly in creating a new national culture. To this end, he founded the *Dürerbund,* an organization to actively further art in education and everyday life, the care of the environment, and support progressive tendencies in the development of the arts. [62]

An offshoot of this initiative emerged at a *Dürerbund* conference on contemporary architecture held at Erfurt in 1903, which in March, 1904, crystallized as the *Bund für Heimatschutz* (Society for Protection of the Homeland). [63] Its president was Paul Schultze-Naumburg, an architect and head of an art-school in Saaleck, who had regularly written articles on architecture, applied art and craft, and the environment for *Kunstwart*. Under his leadership, the *Heimatschutz* soon became a powerful force in publicizing environmental problems and a focus for all dedicated to preserving the traditional fabric and life of Germany. It grew rapidly, by its second conference in 1906 claiming 100,000 people were involved through individual or corporate membership.

An example of its activities was the *Verein für Niedersächsisches Volkstum* (Association for Lower Saxon Folklore) of Bremen which functioned as a self-governing affiliate of the *Heimatschutz*, emphasizing its local region. It sought to protect old buildings and submitted designs for new projects; organized lectures on folk art and exhibitions of characteristic regional craft-work, both ancient and contemporary; among several working groups was one establishing a collection of regional applied art for the Kunstgewerbemuseum, Bremen. The group worked to preserve and promote those remaining crafts not yet fallen victim to industrialization and to create new forms in the spirit of any that had been lost.

The range of institutions and ideas which emerged was clear evidence of the dynamic engendered by the concept of cultural reform. If, initially, it was a body of theory in search of suitable forms of practice, by the 1890s a growing body of work in the applied arts had broken away from historical revivalism, inspired largely by naturalism and a variety of influences from abroad. This work has often been overshadowed by later developments, but the creation of a visual vocabulary as an alternative to historicism, and of a public receptive to new design concepts, was no mean achievement.

One of the most outstanding figures was Hans von Berlepsch, who was born in 1852 in Switzerland. His father had fled from Germany as a refugee following the 1848 revolutions and later became well-known for his publications on nature and landscape in the Alps. Through his father, the young Berlepsch gained an intimate knowledge of natural forms. In 1868 he commenced the study of architecture at Zurich Polytechnic under Gottfried Semper, who, particularly through his emphasis on materials as the mainspring of creativity, had a profound influence, indeed thirty years later von Berlepsch could say, 'He still does today'. [64] Semper's teachings subsequently led him to work as a carpenter and builder, to gain practical experience, which he combined with the study of history and archaeology. On completing his studies he worked for a time as architect and illustrator, but in 1876 decided to study painting at the Munich Academy. Subsequently, he travelled widely in Europe and the Middle East, and experimented with work in a variety of materials, in both two and three dimensions. By the early 1880s he was beginning to concentrate on applied art and write articles calling for its regeneration, for a rejection of historicism and a return to a recognition of natural forms, as means of clearing away the accumulated burden of scholarship and fashion and returning to the original source of all art. An exhibition of Japanese work in 1885 at Nuremburg excited his interest, with its respect for materials and an absence of plastic effects and acceptance of flat surfaces. From this time he worked in a very wide range of materials for diverse purposes, textiles, metalwork, ceramics and furniture. His structures were basically simple, solid forms with a fundamental geometric emphasis. A rich effect was created by the

Wrought-iron candle-holder by Hans von Berlepsch shown at the Munich International Exhibition of Art, 1897.

A document cabinet by Hans von Berlepsch exhibited in Munich in 1898. Of basically simple construction, it used surface pattern for decorative purposes, rather than the addition of extraneous forms.

The firms of Buyten & Söhne, for whom Hans von Berlepsch frequently designed, and Georg Schöttle of Stuttgart, held the German rights to a patented method of relief patterning of timber surfaces known as Xylektopom, here advertised in 1898 for its value in producing 'furniture in the modern style ... designed by prominent artists.' (courtesy: RIBA)

natural decorative motifs which although often complex, never overpowered the basic structure, but were always contained within it. For Berlepsch, a separation of construction and decoration did not come into consideration, his purpose was always to integrate both into a total expression that enhanced the function of an object, and raised it beyond the purely utilitarian. However, it took many years for him to gain full recognition, which did not come until his work was shown at the Munich International Exhibition of Art in 1897, when it was widely publicized in contemporary journals at home and abroad. The exhibition was predominantly of fine art, but though small, the applied art section had a greater impact. *The Studio's* Munich correspondent wrote: 'I must, however, draw attention to the couple of small yet capacious rooms in which modern applied art asserts itself publically and formally for the first time in Munich. These two narrow apartments, decorated with a healthy and refined taste, hold out perhaps more promise for the future than any in the whole exhibition . . .' [65] Berlepsch was suddenly recognized as one of the foremost artists 'who have been instrumental in promoting and furthering the new industrial art movement in Germany' [66], and one of the pioneers who 'breached the gap and placed themselves on the summit' [67], though he has subsequently been neglected in many accounts of this period.

Berlepsch's designs were executed by a number of firms with whom he worked in close co-operation, for example the furniture

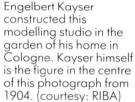

Engelbert Kayser constructed this modelling studio in the garden of his home in Cologne. Kayser himself is the figure in the centre of this photograph from 1904. (courtesy: RIBA)

Advertisement from 1899 for the firm of Kayser of Cologne, emphasizing traditional values in the manufacture of *Kayserzinn* (silver-pewter) products in which the firm specialized. (courtesy: RIBA)

Fish-serving dish in silver pewter by Engelbert Kayser, 1897. Like most of Kayser's designs this uses natural motifs as an integral part of the conception.

Serving-dish designed by Engelbert Kayser c.1900 in silver pewter with a relief pattern of ivy leaves. (courtesy: Alksnis Collection, Geneva)

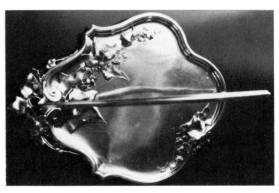

manufacturer, Buyten & Söhne of Düsseldorf. However, many companies also began to develop initiatives of their own. The metalware workshop founded by J.P. Kayser had grown by 1885 to a large factory situated at Oppum, near Krefeld. In 1880 the company had established an 'Arts and Crafts section for luxury utensils' which used outside artists as advisors, though the majority of the companies products, useful wares, were designed by draughtsmen and modellers who were full-time employees. In 1890 an art workshop was established in Cologne under the leadership of Engelbert Kayser, son of the founder, to unite the design of luxury and useful goods under one roof and co-ordinate internal and external contributions. The designs from the workshop together with those of notable consultants, such as the architect, Karl Geyer, rapidly gained a high reputation, mainly for

work in *Kayser-Zinn,* a pewter alloy developed by Engelbert giving a matt and silvery surface of pleasing appearance, which was sometimes used alone, sometimes with crystal. Since there was no lead in the alloy it was particularly suitable for table use and drinking vessels, indeed Engelbert Kayser was credited with designing and modelling the first 'modern' beer-tankard in 1894. Like Berlepsch, the keynote of Kayser's work was a clearly defined functional form on which motifs derived from nature, plants, leaves, insects and flowers, were used as surface decoration, though sometimes on more decorative pieces, the natural forms themselves formed the basis of the design. This integration of ornament and utility was seen as its great virtue. 'And so the many kinds of vessels, containers, bowls and dishes are able . . . to serve as show-pieces, and also in

Double-gourd shaped vase by Max Läuger, produced before 1900 by the Tonwerk Kandem for which he was artistic director. (courtesy: Badisches Landesmuseum, Karlsruhe)

Chimney surround in beaten copper by Max Läuger, exhibited at the Jubilee Art Exhibition in Karlsruhe, 1902.

A similar approach characterized the work of Max Läuger, who from 1888 taught studies in stylization from nature at the Karlsruhe School of Applied Art, and developed the concepts derived from his teaching in ceramic wares. Again, the forms were simple and well-proportioned, using colour and decorative forms from nature within the limits of the structure. Läuger's work later broadened to include posters, interior decoration, and by 1898, cast-iron surrounds for gas-fires produced by Friedrich Siemens of Dresden and other companies.

In one sense, the work of such individuals could be argued to anticipate the role of modern designers in industry, both as consultant and in-house designer. There were essential differences, however, which require such assessments to be made with caution. Berlepsch, Kayser and Läuger all considered themselves artists, and their designs were for craft-production. Indeed, the popularity Läuger's ceramics began to enjoy in the late 1890s caused considerable problems for him. Since he considered the design of any product having claims to artistic quality must originate in the workshop and be conditioned by the materials used, in other words, artistic possibility was restricted to craft techniques, it was extremely difficult to increase production and adequately meet demand. It should also be noted that by the end of the first decade of the twentieth century, Kayser Söhne were in deep financial and commercial crisis due to their craft-based production coming under severe competitive pressure from mechanized manufacture. If their achievement and that of others like them is assessed in its own terms, however, in the context of the period around 1890, then it appears far more significant. By emphasizing the quality and integrity of materials and workmanship, and in their synthetic view of function and artistry, they established concepts in practice which challenged the prevailing taste for historicism and opened the eyes of at least a section of the public to

respect of their practical utilization at the table to satisfy as objects of use. This is not a deprecatory meaning, for in it lies a cardinal virtue of the so-called modern style: an object should not only be attractive and pleasing, but also functional and useable.'[68]

Alexander Koch.

Title-page from an 1890 issue of the journal Innen-Dekoration published by Alexander Koch of Darmstadt. This continued the practice of emphasizing the decorative bounty provided by buxom goddesses of art, though by the late 1890s, the journal adopted a more restrained approach. (courtesy: RIBA)

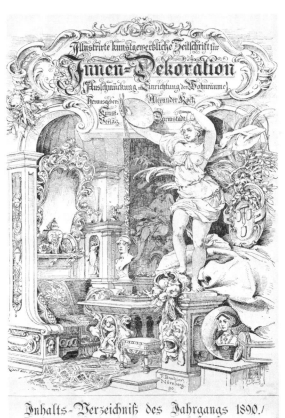

new possibilities.

A crucial factor in that growth of public recognition was the appearance of three new journals dedicated to the applied arts. *The Studio,* first published in Britain in 1893, is often assumed to be the forerunner of such magazines, but in fact it was preceded by *Innendekoration,* published and edited by Alexander Koch in Darmstadt, in 1891. In its early years it mirrored the contemporary preoccupation with stylistic concerns, its pages running the gamut of historical and national models. By the mid-1890s, however, Koch became convinced of the need for forms expressive of cultural values that represented modern Germany, and the emphasis in *Innendekoration* changed sharply. In 1897, he founded a second, companion publication

with a wider frame of reference, *Deutsche Kunst und Dekoration,* and in the same year, in Munich, there appeared *Dekorative Kunst,* edited by H. Bruckmann and Julius Meier-Graaf. In contrast to longer established journals with their overwhelming emphasis on historical scholarship, these three newcomers were dedicated to promoting the work of their age, and in contrast to *The Studio,* which increasingly concentrated on fine art, vigorously promoted applied art and design, with extensive discussions of both theory and practice. They used advanced printing techniques, including occasionally colour, to create a modern image. In the first issue of *Deutsche Kunst und Dekoration,* Alexander Koch addressed his first editorial 'To German artists and artlovers'. His opening was dramatic: 'More than ever the practice of art in the Fatherland again appears dependent upon England, America and France . . . the idiom of an indigenous, individual German art language threatens to become lost!' The reason for this was attributed to the concept of applied art, which created second-class artists. Could there be, exclaimed Koch, 'Really great artists for the — minor arts!' There was indeed a need for an inter-penetration of all the arts. 'This demand is not synonymous with the war-cry: "Away with everything old" of the radical innovators; but a whole series of new discoveries and equipment, new raw materials, new techniques require also a contemporary form and development befitting it only from true artistic hands.'

The purpose of the journal was therefore declared to be the promotion of true German art, to bring to the attention of the world the achievements of German art, and 'indeed, to help achieve the victory of Germany and the lands of German tongue in competition with other nations!' [69]

The theme of what kind of emphasis was needed in German art was further elaborated in the same issue in an article entitled

'Changeable furniture' designed by Wilhelm Michael of Munich, which won first prize in a competition organized by Alexander Koch and was prominently featured in the Darmstadt Art and Applied Art Exhibition of 1898. The components could be assembled in varying configurations to suit different needs or surroundings. (courtesy: RIBA)

'National Art — Necessary Art' by Hans Schliepmann. He began by drawing a distinction between 'the arts of intellect', which dominate in an age of science and technology, and 'the true art, the creative activity of imagination and feeling' which has less space. Art, he asserted, is one of the most original needs of men and in a true culture permeates all aspects of life, and is not therefore 'an expensive luxury'. To create a new public and new ideas would not be easy, therefore 'art must above all be effective in the design of everyday needs . . . We cannot begin with Faust, the Ninth Symphony and the Sistine Chapel, in order to awaken an understanding of art, a joy in art; but from our daily

environment it shall allure us ever higher . . . Therefore for us the most necessary art is above all not the so-called high art, but that which one has sadly deprecatingly called applied art . . .' What was needed, concluded Schliepmann, was a real art of beautiful simplicity that speaks of modern life to a modern generation, with full respect for ancient art as much as modern consciousness. This would create a new German art that would also have economic advantages. The state must play a role in promoting it, but so too must industry: 'a nervous, overstrained servant of Mammon must become a master of Mammon.' [70]

The role Alexander Koch intended to play was not simply one of reportage and exhortation, but also where possible, direct participation. At a major Art and Applied Art Exhibition held in Darmstadt in 1898, the organization and direction of the applied art section was given over to the editors of *Deutsche Kunst und Dekoration*, who attempted to exhibit 'middle-class rooms of modern art character', with the purpose of 'awakening in the public a feeling for the German way and German character in contemporary art.' Prominence was given to the Blue Room by Wilhelm Michael, a Munich designer, in which the furniture was constructed on a system conceived by Koch. This 'changeable furniture' was intended for 'those educated circles' dependent upon rented accommodation who yet wanted 'original, pleasant and artistic interior spaces.' The range of pieces included an extendable table, chairs, a sofa, upholstered benches, a book-case with writing surface, two high cupboards, a corner-cupboard with mirror and several smaller pieces. They could be assembled in varying combinations to suit different ground-plans and fenestration, and to demonstrate their potential, the pieces were rearranged at intervals during the exhibition in different configurations, for different purposes, reception-, dining- or smoking room. The construction of the pieces was sound and straightforward in stained oak with minimal decoration and metal fittings. [71] Another feature of Koch's attempts to promote new ideas, was a series of competitions for designs organized by his journals, for various items of household furnishings and fittings. The range of books and folios he published on the applied arts was also one of the main instruments of increasing public awareness of new developments.

In another practical initiative of this period, which emerged as one of the most significant design institutions in the movement for cultural reform, the influence of developments in England can be detected. The ideas of Ruskin were widely known. Indeed, after a visit to England in 1911, Theodor Heuss felt that Ruskin's ideological influence had been greater in Germany than in his homeland. [72] The efforts of William Morris in establishing a company to realize these ideals and similar subsequent initiatives by members of the Arts and Crafts Movement such as C.R. Ashbee with his Guild of Handicraft established in London in 1889, also provided a model for emulation.

The pattern of craft business established by Morris and Ashbee would seem to have inspired the establishment of the *Dresdener Werkstätten für Handwerkskunst* (the Dresden Workshops for Arts and Crafts). Founded at Hellerau, near Dresden, by Karl Schmidt in 1898, following his return from a year in England after completing his apprenticeship as a carpenter, and set up with two assistants, it rapidly expanded. A foundation manifesto published in 1899 stated its purpose as: 'We want to create furniture, which is so formed, that each piece of domestic furniture directly serves best its purpose and gives expression in its form to its purpose. And further, people shall see in our furniture, that it is prepared from German materials, created by German artists, and is the expression of German emotions and feelings.' [73]

Karl Schmidt had a deep sense of tradition,

but for him the past was a source of inspiration requiring re-interpretation in contemporary terms if its validity in national life was to be maintained. From the beginning he sought to enlist the co-operation of artists, amongst the first of whom in 1899 were Ernst Walther and J.V. Cizzarz, both painters, a sculptor, Karl Gross, and an architect, Wilhelm Kreis. Their names were advertised with their designs, they were encouraged to supervise production and were given a share of the profits. Whilst part of his early production was high-quality hand-crafted work, Schmidt also set out to produce more modest furniture at lower prices. In a furniture exhibition in Dresden in 1899, two complete sets of fittings for living, bedroom and kitchen won prizes, one by Karl Gross and the other by Gertrud and Erich Kleinhempel, costing a total of 800 & 750 Reichmarks respectively. [74]

Schmidt's initiative can, in many respects, be regarded as a practical culmination of many of the preoccupations and endeavours that had engaged so much effort in the previous quarter-century, and it was to further develop in the early twentieth century as one of the most significant institutions of the cultural reform movement.

6 Jugendstil

A further initiative which emerged in the 1890s was the German variant of *Art Nouveau*, known as *Jugendstil* (Style of Youth). This differed from most other tendencies in that its origins and development were strongly cosmopolitan, though national variants did emerge and in Germany it eventually became part of the cultural reform movement. A common feature was the intention to create wholly new forms representative of the age, and it thus marked a significant rejection of the constant reference to historical precedent which dominated nineteenth century visual culture. Most fundamentally, however, its aim was not only the creation of a new style, but the transformation of everyday life in all its aspects. To achieve this, nothing was too great or too small to be worthy of aesthetic concern, and the applied arts consequently became a central concern of the movement. Its characteristics therefore matched the aspirations of the cultural reformers in Germany, and *Jugendstil*, although only a passing phase, was to make an enormous contribution to it in terms of practice.

The artistic origins of *Art Nouveau* were diverse and sometimes obscure, including amongst its influences mediaeval decoration, the Arts and Crafts movement, Japanese artefacts, naturalism and symbolism in painting. It came to Germany from France and Belgium comparatively late, and although *Jugendstil* initially adopted the two-dimensional linear techniques and natural forms typical of *Art Nouveau* in those countries, influenced by the Viennese Secessionists, it evolved by 1900 a more angular repertoire of forms emphasizing constructive rather than decorative possibilities.

The main centre of the movement in Germany was Munich, where in the early 1890s, it attracted a group of artists dissatis-fied with official academic style and the prevailing pomp. Graphic art provided an easy means of transition from fine to applied art for many, and journals such as *Pan* and *Jugend* provided a ready outlet. This later led to an exploration of the possibilities of furniture, glass and ceramics, textiles, metalware and eventually architecture, a progression from individual items through to ensembles and whole environments. It was through such a progression that young artists such as Otto Eckmann, August Endell and Peter Behrens began a lifetime's practice in applied art and design. The clearest embodiment of this trend, however, was the foundation in Munich in 1897 of the *Vereinigte Werkstätten für Kunst im Handwerk* (United Workshops for Art in Craftwork) by Hermann Obrist, Bernhard Pankok, Paul Schultze-Naumburg, Richard Riemerschmid and Bruno Paul. The *Vereinigte Werkstätten* was formed with the purpose of obtaining admission for applied art products into the International Art Exhibition held in the Munich Glaspalast in 1897. Its inspiration was the Arts and Crafts ideal of a community of craftsmen with their own workshops, able to produce a full range of everyday objects and so stamp daily life with an integral artistic unity. Its early exhibitions were generally well-received and the *Werkstätten* was soon organized into a limited liability company. The commercial direction of the undertaking by F.A.O. Krüger was perhaps one of the most crucial factors in the transition from the original association to a highly successful commercial venture of considerable size and a prominent centre for quality products.

A feature of the *Vereinigte Werkstätten*, *as well as* those at Hellerau, was that artists were not expected to be executants, indeed one of its purposes was to make available different kinds of technical skill to enable the realization

Music saloon designed by Richard Riemerschmid for the Vereinigte Werkstätten, and exhibited at the German Art Exhibition, Dresden in 1899. The simple elegance of this furniture, emphasizing structure and materials, black/grey water oak, was widely praised and marked a turning point in Riemerschmid's evolution away from the influence of *Jugendstil* curvilinear form. (courtesy: RIBA)

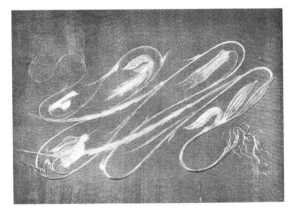

Tapestry *Alpenveilchen* by Herman Obrist, 1895. The vehement line into which Obrist contorted this pattern of the cyclamen plant has led to it frequently being dubbed the 'Whiplash' by critics. It was one of the most extreme examples of curvilinear *Jugendstil*.

English forerunners, such as C.R. Ashbee's Guild of Handicraft, which foundered on its own ideals, in neglect of commercial considerations. In contrast, the thriving German workshops stimulated a wave of emulation. In 1899, *Deutsche Kunst und Dekoration* reported that excited by the success of the *Vereinigte Werkstätten*, 'also a series of other Munich firms attempted to manufacture objects in the new style to artistic designs, and to allow the designer to participate in the profit.' [75] Considerable interest had been aroused by the high quality of the *Werkstätten's* four rooms exhibited at a Dresden exhibition of that year, particularly Richard Riemerschmid's 'Room for a Music Lover'. This showed an assurance and inventiveness in a range of furnishings which revealed a new level of understanding of materials and their formal possibilities, reaching beyond the programmatic aesthetics of *Jugendstil* that Riemerschmid was soon to abandon. The experience of being able to work in close co-operation with the executant craftsmen had obviously brought considerable benefit and is perhaps a crucial reason in explaining the rapid development and progress of the *Werkstätten*.

The formal development of early Munich *Jugendstil* can be illustrated by the work of Hermann Obrist. After studying natural sciences at Heidelberg and applied art at Karlsruhe, he established a tapestry workshop in Florence before moving to Munich in 1894. His tapestry 'Alpine violet' of 1895 was typical of early *Jugendstil*: a two-dimensional piece, the natural theme abstracted and drawn out into powerful linear forms, creating a dynamic whiplash pattern. The dining-room furniture of 1898 for the Heiseler family indicated his exploration of new materials and functions and was much more restrained. Curvilinear elements were still evident, but exploited in the context of structural qualities, with decoration reconciled to function.

If Munich was the cradle of *Jugendstil*, it proved, however, to be an unsympathetic

of artistic ideas, and ensure artistic control over the processes of production. Krüger's direction ensured that commercial success was similarly exploited to ensure the artists' interests were protected. The Morrisian model might have been the starting point, but in their realization, the two main German manifestations of it showed a far greater flexibility and realism. Consequently they had a longer existence and more successful influence than

Furniture in bog oak designed by Hermann Obrist c.1898 for the Haesler family in which curvilinear tendencies are restrained by structural function.

environment in which the new movement could grow. To a considerable extent it provoked opposition. Satirical journals associated with the movement, such as *Jugend* and *Simplicissimus,* constantly excited the wrath of the Bavarian authorities, and the artistic establishment in Munich was antagonized by the utopian claims and the undoubted success of *Jugendstil.* After 1900, the group gathered in Munich began to disperse as the movement there lost impetus.

By that time Otto Eckmann had already left for Berlin, where in 1898 he established a workshop on Hermann Hirschfeld's premises. The latter had become a convert to *Jugendstil* and in the year following Eckmann's arrival, in what was a considerable coup, secured the services of one of Europe's outstanding *Art Nouveau* theorists and practitioners, when the Belgian, Henry van der Velde arrived to take over leadership of the studios and workshops at the Hohenzollern-Kunstgewerbehaus. For several years, Hirschwald's gallery continued to promote *Jugendstil,* in 1903, for example, presenting work by Lalique, a review of *Jugendstil* graphics, and a large major exhibition of the Vienna Workshops.

The style also had adherents in other centres, such as Dresden, where an exhibition by Samuel Bing's *Art Nouveau* gallery from Paris caused great excitement in 1898,

Hamburg and the Rhineland.

The wider aims of *Jugendstil* for a fundamental change in the role of art in everyday life remained unrealized, however, for the same reasons that a national style failed to crystallize. There was simply no broad social consensus to sustain such a sweeping change. Otto Eckmann once wrote: 'We must use the snob, in order to gradually reach the people.' [76] But *Jugendstil* artists never broke their dependence on rich patrons to establish this broader base of support. It was ironic in view of their ambitions, that what at the same time was both the apogee and the swansong of *Jugendstil* should be an artists' colony established at Darmstadt by Grand Duke Ernst Ludwig of Hesse in 1899. This provided the opportunity and funds for a group of artists to live and work in Darmstadt.

Alexander Koch, who was closely involved with the creation of the colony, emphasized in an article introducing it, that its concern would be the applied and decorative arts. The crafts, he stated, could only survive through artistic and personal qualities 'in which intelligence, taste, unique ideas and the highest possible indigenous spirit are given expression. The machine cannot do that. Neither can every craftsman.' The less able craftsmen would therefore have to work in factories, but the more talented could be helped if close links between artists and craftsmen were established. In co-operation they could influence public taste, carrying the artistic expression of the German spirit into the homes of the populace. Koch concluded '. . . an advancement of modern applied art is synonymous with a raising of the propaganda power of the nation.' [77]

This emphasis on the crafts, national identity and economic success, and reform from above percolating downwards in society, was part of the mainstream of contemporary thought, but the Darmstadt colony was unusual in being emphatically linked to the patronage of an enlightened ruler.

Design for a vase by Adolf Seder of Munich, 1871. The combination of abstract, natural and heraldic forms typifies the eclectism of this period.

Six scent bottles by H. Wichmann, 1873, using a diversity of decorative motifs for fashionable effect.

Moderne Blumenvase.
Entwurf von Architekt Hans Friedel, München.

A domestic heating stove by Rudolf Seitz, 1877. In the nineteenth century the traditional tiled oven evolved into a decorative focal point, losing many of its ancillary functions, such as cooking, in the process.

This design by the architect Hans Friedel of Munich, dating from 1896, was described as a 'modern flower vase'. The comparatively restricted surface decoration of simple abstract patterns and the integration of decorative and functional elements were typical of efforts to define a contemporary design style.

Music room, Behrens House, Darmstadt.

Peter Behrens' house constructed on the Mathildenhöhe, Darmstadt in 1901-2. This was the first major architectural project undertaken by Behrens.

Hallway of the Behrens House, Darmstadt.

Young girl's bedroom, Behrens House, Darmstadt.

Mantelpiece, Behrens
House, Darmstadt.

The artists participating were invited on the basis of individual talents, which collectively spanned a wide range of possible applications. The painter Hans Christiansen and the engraver and medallist Rudolf Bosselt were recalled from Paris, Patriz Huber, an interior designer came from Munich, as did Paul Burck, who specialized in weaving and embroidery. These four arrived in July, 1899, to be joined later in the year by a sculptor, Ludwig Habbich, Peter Behrens, and from Vienna, Josef-Maria Olbrich. The personnel changed over the years, with over twenty being active members at various times before 1914.

The major project of its early years, and most lasting memorial, was the design and construction of a series of public buildings and artists' dwellings on a hill-top site, the Mathildenhöhe, above the city. The major contribution here was by Olbrich, whose architectural training and experience in Vienna gave him an assurance that exercised a profound influence on the other members, though the fact of being Austrian led to his contribution sometimes being undervalued, by Alexander Koch in particular. Peter Behrens, who was enabled to venture into the realm of architecture for the first time in designing his own house, must have learnt much from Olbrich. In Behrens' interiors, there was a move away from the curving fluidity of early *Jugendstil*, to a use of more restrained lines in which geometrical motifs in repetitive patterns typical of Viennese practice, came to play a more emphatic part, as in the ladies' room and kitchen. The motifs might have been simplified, but in many respects, however, the materials used were often lavish. In the music-room, the most dramatic of Behrens designs, the walls were clad with inlaid woods of varying shades, with a marble-clad niche, blue glass mirrors and a gilded ceiling, which led one observer to protest, since 'Honesty and simplicity in the use of materials are the primary conditions of modern art

handicraft'.[78] Behrens himself emphasized the combination of two elements: '... that of practical utility and that of abstract beauty ...', though it was the latter which had primary importance. 'This development of artistic perception, combined with the progress made in our technique and the newly discovered materials, is at once a guarantee of the fertility of the modern style and its justification.'[79]

Behrens stress on artistry, and the highly individual nature of his house, and that of the others simultaneously constructed, can hardly be seen to fulfil the original aims of the colony as set out by Koch. At the exhibition in 1902 for which the houses were completed, a sharp contrast was drawn with the work of Patriz Huber, in which was evident 'the conviction

Bedroom designed by Patriz Huber for the exhibition of the Darmstadt Artists Colony, 1901.

that simple middle-class furniture may be produced which will meet middle-class requirements . . . In the first place the artist is conscious of the fact that he is raising dwellings and designing furniture for ordinary men. He begins by excluding extravagance in colour and outline. His aim is comfort combined with agreeable effect. Of course, he is also endeavouring to found a new style. Only he seeks his effects less by designing rooms strongly individual — individual, that is, as regards the inmates — than by inventing new forms for typical furniture . . . In this essential difference between Patriz Huber and Behrens and Olbrich, as well as many other modern architects of interiors, lies a good deal of Huber's special distinctiveness.' [80] Certainly the nature of his work was different to his Darmstadt colleagues, however it was considered most suitable for the middle classes of medium and small towns. The types he conceived were therefore limited to a specific social context. This was not unusual, given that the initiative for cultural reform stemmed

to a large extent from the middle classes. The distinction, however, between individualism expressed in aesthetic terms, and the satisfaction of general needs by the creation of typical forms was to become a major focus of debate in the first decade of the new century.

The Darmstadt experiment enabled the *Jugendstil* ideas of ensemble, both interior and exterior, to be realized on a hitherto unprecedented scale; but the predominant individualism, together with the fact that it was an artistic island dependent upon aristocratic patronage, made it the subject of considerable criticism. In the *Deutsche Bauzeitung*, an architectural journal of conventional views, one of its editors, Albert Hoffmann mordantly caricatured the ethos of the colony as: 'from us and our school beams everything shining and redemptive, the path we have beaten is "the" new path, our art is alone art, which mankind has long hoped for with consuming longing . . . ' [81] This, in Hoffmann's opinion, did not correspond with the needs of the time. Whilst recognizing the achievements of Olbrich, 'a brilliant comet . . . that threatens to become extinguished the more brightly it burns . . . ' [82], his work was considered an exotic growth transplanted in alien soil — there was little doubt too of Hoffmann's prejudice against Olbrich's Viennese origins. Behrens' house was felt to be a ' . . . rejection of real life, transcendentalism almost bordering on the pathological . . . ' and his art 'a strong strand of ascetic-hieratic disposition, with a shimmer of mystical gloss.' [83] Seen in the light of the objective needs of ordinary people, the colony was a 'soaring Icarus flight into the romantic land of ideal art practice' [84], and doomed to crash down on the enduring ground of reality, though Hoffmann also finally conceded another point of view, that of a burning protest of youth, an assertion of its creative power against a constricting artistic legacy and philistinism, even though such romanticism was 'sadly, sadly past'.

Hoffman saw little future for *Jugendstil*, and

Smoking-set in cast brass by WMF, c.1905. Such sets provided all the requisites of a smoker on formal occasions. (courtesy: Alksnis Collection, Geneva)

Wine-jug with silver-plated mountings in *Jugendstil* style by the Würtemburgische Metalfabrik (WMF), c.1900. (courtesy: Alksnis Collection, Geneva)

Wine goblet, silver-plated by WMF, c.1900. (courtesy: Alksnis Collection, Geneva)

in that respect his perception was accurate. *Jugendstil* survived into the 1900s, but increasingly as a series of decorative motifs appropriated by manufacturers as one style amongst many. A prominent example was the *Würtemburgische Metallfabrik* (WMF). The origins of this firm dated back to 1853 when Daniel Straub formed a company to produce metalwares at Geislingen, though it only assumed the title of WMF after an amalgamation with other companies in 1888. To the production of a broad range of metal goods, in silver, nickel, copper, brass and pewter, was subsequently added the facility to manufacture crystal and glass. It was a highly successful company, employing some 3000 workers by the turn of the century and with sales outlets in many European countries. The styles of its products were in the mainstream of the historical revivals fashionable at the time, varying from Old German to Renaissance and Rococo, but in the years after 1900, *Jugendstil* came to play a predominant role. WMF's ability to produce goods in a range and in quantities far exceeding the possibilities of craft workshops gave it a market advantage it was quick to exploit, and its capacity for both metal and glass were suc-

cessfully combined in a series of wine jugs and goblets, as well as purely metal items, such as ornamental dishes, plate and centre-pieces in silvered metal and pewter. The quality of such produce varied, at its best revealing a sympathetic understanding of the style allied to the technical competence of the company, this generally in wares requiring a high input of skilled labour. Other goods, such as stamped dishes which lent themselves to mass-production displayed less sensitivity and commercial opportunity was clearly the motivation behind them. Yet by such means *Jugendstil* became accessible to a wider market, though in a manner over which its originators had no control. Since it was precisely this experience of involvement in and control over production that had been considered of greatest benefit in the movement, it was hardly surprising that many practitioners who emerged in the *Jugendstil* period were subsequently vehement in asserting the demands of artists over the requirements of industry.

There were, undoubtedly, indulgent and delusory aspects of *Jugendstil*. Its positive results, however, were considerable, and none more so than the grounding it gave to a

Glasses designed by Hans Christiansen, a member of the Darmstadt colony, for the Theresientaler Krystallglasfabrik, 1901-7. (courtesy: Badisches Landesmuseum, Karlsruhe)

Candelabra designed by Friedrich Adler and executed by the Giesserei Walter Scherf of Nuremberg, 1901. (courtesy: Badisches Landesmuseum, Karlsruhe)

youthful body of talent who were to provide a continuing and rich contribution to the evolution of German design. It was also a fertile source of concepts which later evolved to become part of the mainstream of design ideas. Short-lived it might have been, but it was part of a vital ground-swell from which the imbalance between theory and practice began to be redressed and some, at least, of the programmatic aims of the cultural reform movement saw practical realization in a continually widening range of activities.

However, although the social emphasis of the majority of those involved in *Jugendstil* was liberal or conservative, nationalist and middle-class, its achievements were also capable of a very different interpretation. In a series of articles inspired by *Jugendstil* and written around the turn of the century, a Polish socialist working in Germany, Julian Marchlewski, argued that the applied art movement was a revolution in the visual arts, 'and it appears to us thoroughly logical that the first banner carriers of the revolution — were socialists.'[85] Morris was the obvious example, but colleagues such as Walter Crane, Burne-Jones, Sedding, Cobden-Sanderson and others who shared his convictions were also cited. They, it was argued, had exposed the ugliness of manufactured products and established the principle that articles corresponding to contemporary life and needs should be created, on the basis that not the costliness of materials counted, but to so form materials that their beauty became visible.

Marchlewski's views differed essentially from these English exemplars, however, in regard to mechanization. 'The matter stands thus: the domestic equipment we usually need today is cheap because it is made by machines. Where then is it written, that one must make only ugly objects with machines? No, the thing that matters is to conceive forms that are beautiful and thoroughly correspond to the technology. The machine is not to blame for objects being detestable. On the contrary: the objects are detestable because they are manufactured by machines, but so appear as if they were not machine work.'[86] In that point of view,

Coffee- and tea-service
by Albin Müller for
Gerhardi & Co of
Nuremberg, c.1905.
(courtesy: Badisches
Landesmuseum,
Karlsruhe)

Marchlewski acknowledged the influence of by Henry van der Velde, whose advocacy of socialism followed Morris, though with less of a revolutionary emphasis and an intellectual acceptance, at least, of technology and mechanization as a contemporary creative force.

Marchlewski linked these ideas of the new applied art in relation to mechanization to a fundamental critique of the economic structure of contemporary society. 'It is the old story: the machine is not guilty for the distress, the poor quality and the useless ugliness of products, but the capitalistic form of applying the machine.' [87] And in that form, the profit motive was culprit, with manufacturers unscrupulously exploiting the market. 'Because their greatest profit comes from the production of junk goods, so they produce junk goods.' [88] In order to effect a change which would enable the potential of the machine to be beneficiently applied, it was therefore necessary to change society. 'The machine as a tool does not preclude beauty, on the contrary, it should and can essentially support men in the production of beautiful objects. The machine is not a tool of exploitation by nature, but corresponds to its social relationships.' [89] Here Marx was explicitly referred to, and his influence was also apparent in Marchlewski's conclusion: 'As soon as the relationships alter, so also the aesthetic function of the machine alters.' [90]

The components of Marchlewski's arguments were hardly new, but the primacy of social change which he stressed inverted the whole thrust of most discussion of the applied arts at the end of the nineteenth century, in which aesthetic change was the decisive element. Though given varying emphasis — the recreation of the past, economic competitiveness, cultural status, social unification or moral regeneration — the desired ends were generally envisaged within the social status quo. The implications might be radical, but were not revolutionary. Little attention was paid to the needs and aspirations of the working classes, other than as an extension of the perceptions of other social groups, in all the nuances of debate over cultural reform. Indeed, one of the most interesting features of Marchlewski's arguments was the extent to which he drew on that debate to reach very different, if for the time, atypical conclusions. This was itself an indication of the extent to which the middle classes, denied effective political power, had asserted themselves strongly in cultural initiatives and established a powerful hold over this sphere in the years since unification. By the turn of the century their confidence was growing.

In any historical study the precise identification of decisive shifts in general consciousness is invariably problematic, rarely dovetailing with convenient patterns of chronology. Therefore, when considering ideas significant in the evolution of German design, the choice of 1900 to indicate a turning point has only limited validity and must be hedged with qualifications. Yet for many Germans, particularly those born around the period of unification and coming to maturity by the turn of the century, there was indeed a sense of being poised on the threshold of a new era. No sudden transformation resulted, for time is necessary to translate awareness of possibility into effective action, but over the following decade there was a release of energy, the creative momentum of a generation who believed the twentieth century would belong to them and to Germany.

7 The Role of Government

The tradition of government inherited by the Reich, indeed the social cohesiveness of Germany, hinged upon the subordination of individuality (which is not necessarily synonymous with its repression) to the community as represented by the state. The constitutional structure of the state was a hierarchical pyramid with power concentrated at the apex, ministers being ultimately responsible to the Emperor rather than the elected parliament, the Reichstag. Policy thus devolved through a highly-trained and efficient bureaucracy rather than the elected representatives, with the state intervening widely in activities it wished to promote or saw in its interests. The result was not dictatorship, but rather a heavy-handed, autocratic paternalism, in which conformity was expected and generally conceded.

Under such a system, the patronage the Reich government and public bodies at all levels exercised was considerable, covering such forms as buildings, monuments, currency and postage stamps, uniforms and street furniture. Indirectly, the taste of the Emperor and court filtered down through the channels of government agencies, manifesting itself generally in a ponderous, highly-decorated symbolism drawing heavily on German mythology and a mélange of historical forms.

The aesthetic predilections of the theatrical Emperor Wilhelm II can be easily derided, but it would be a mistake to underestimate the influence of his authority, given the power structure of which he was head.

Senior appointments to the major art institutions of the capital were subject to his approval and the appointment of Wilhelm von Bode as General Director of Berlin's Museums in 1906 owed as much to his friendship with the Emperor as to his undoubted abilities. The main interest of the Emperor was in archaeology, where his patronage was generally enlightened and had a beneficent effect. He was completely intolerant of modern art, however, and the negative side of his authority became apparent in 1909, when Hugo Tschudi resigned his directorship of the National Gallery after the Emperor had vetoed the purchase of French Impressionist paintings.

His attitudes were clearly expressed in a speech at the ceremonial opening in 1901 of the Siegesallee, a promenade in Berlin's Tiergarten lined with thirty huge statues of historical figures, a gift from the Emperor to the city. In his address, he equated art with the Ideal, a body of unchanging, eternal values, and castigated any concept of artistic freedom which did not conform to this as a sin against the nation. On the social role of art, he stated: '. . . art should help to educate a nation. . . The great ideals have become the heritage of us, the German nation, while other nations have lost them in greater or lesser

The development of the post-box in Germany. The two above are from Prussia: left, a wooden model from 1850; right, cast-iron, 1860. Lower left, the first cast-iron Riechspost model of 1875; right, a cast-iron and enamelled model of 1892.

degree. Only the German nation is left to follow the vocation of protecting, cherishing and propagating these great ideals, and one of these ideals is that we should give the working, the laborious classes, the opportunity to raise themselves up to what is beautiful and to work their way out of and above their other thoughts.'[91] For Wilhelm II, art was a social narcotic, his Ideal a sentimental confection of decorative embellishment glorifying his regime, bearing little relationship to the realities of the society he ruled. Indeed, perhaps the greatest task then facing the cultural reformers was to educate their monarch.

Fortunately for Germany, however, there were officials at various levels who were more enlightened than their Emperor. With the degree of power and patronage available to public bodies, and in a climate of opinion where visual form was of important representational significance, it could be possible for practitioners to be given considerable scope for innovative development. The Reich government, for example, provided a 'Standing Exhibition Commission for German Industry' under the Ministry of the Interior, which included representatives from the Foreign Ministry, the Prussian Ministries of Commerce and Education, and other interested parties. This was responsible for the presentation of offical national exhibits at major international exhibitions, the normal method being to appoint a state official as commissioner responsible for the task, and provided direct funding. Subsidies were also available for exhibitions where a direct state involvement was inappropriate. With Germany's emergence as a major political and industrial power, such events were given high priority in the first decade of the century, as a means of impressing the world outside with the nation's strength and achievement, though in the consciousness of officials, this was not necessarily best expressed by new initiatives in architecture and applied art.

If idealism for renewal and change gained a new impulse in 1900, the major event of that year in architecture and design, the World Exposition in Paris, demonstrated that the legacy of the past was not easily jettisoned with a change of calendar. Paris was a special challenge, providing an opportunity to impress the arch-enemy in their own capital. Despite military defeat, the French cultural domination of Europe remained undisputed, a status generally acknowledged in German publications, though usually prefacing a hope of their country soon toppling the French from that supremacy. Some German reporting of the Paris Exposition displayed a distinctly *parvenu* quality in its mixture of arrogance and inferiority: stridently asserting their own power and pride, yet overawed by the assurance of French style and taste, and avidly reporting any compliments on their exhibits culled from the French press.

To design the German pavilion, two established architects were appointed, Karl Hoffacker of Berlin for the structure and Emanuel Seidl of Munich for the ceremonial room. Hoffacker's entrance court was large, flamboyant and intended to impress, essentially a piece of official bombast. Seidl had designed the pavilion for the 1888 *Kunstgewerbe* exhibition in Munich, and his ceremonial rooms showed little development from that earlier event. The decor was lush, with heavy, decorative furniture of obscure stylistic origins and grandiose proportions.

In its more positive aspects, the exhibition was the first major international venture for the *Vereinigte Werkstätten* of Munich. Bruno Paul designed a 'Hunting Room' with furniture in elm and wall-panelling in like materials, the latter surmounted by a marquetry frieze. It was a combination of rectangular and curvilinear forms, of richness and simplicity, the only jarring note being the vehement curves of the chairs which disturbed the general restraint. In contrast, Bernhard Pankok's interior was a more full-blooded and eccen-

The entrance court to the German pavilion at the 1900 Paris Exposition, by Karl Hoffacker. (courtesy: RIBA)

Ceremonial room in the
German pavilion, 1900
Paris Exposition, by
Emanuel Seidl. This
would have been used
for official receptions and
was typical of Seidl's
heavy, monumental style.
(courtesy: RIBA)

Smoking-room by
Bernhard Pankok for the
Vereinigte Werkstätten,
Munich, exhibited at the
Paris Exposition, 1900.

'Room for an Art Lover' by Richard Riemerschmid for the *Vereinigte Werkstätten*, Munich and exhibited at the 1900 Paris Exposition.

Hunting-room by Bruno Paul for *Vereinigte Werkstätten*, Munich, exhibited at the Paris Exposition, 1900.

Darmstadt colony room designed by J-M Olbrich for the German pavilion at the 1900 Paris Exposition. Olbrich also made major contributions to the pavilion of his native Austria.

tric example of curvilinear *Jugendstil* in walnut and cherry. Its sweeping lines, rich materials and of carved ornament created a restless effect. This latter quality was also apparent in Richard Riemerschmid's 'Room of an Art Lover', which had a frieze and ceiling on which the whiplash patterns widely characteristic of *Art Nouveau* were so combined and convoluted as to take on almost frenzied proportions. The furnishings and fittings were by several designers and whilst individual pieces were attractive, the overall effect was heavy, lacking in harmony.

The extent of progress in Germany was apparent from the international interest aroused by the German exhibits. A review by the French critic, Gabriel Mourey, opened by according 'Praise without reserve' for the honesty and excellent ideas 'which almost without exception reveal a truly Germanic sense of decorative art.' Mourey's somewhat stereotyped conception of the 'truly Germanic' had a sting in the tail, however, as subsequently became clear: 'Everything too – which is equally remarkable and commendable – is designedly modern in tendency, that is to say, as modern as it is possible to be, in regard to art, in Germany.' The reason given for this reservation, which contradicted his opening praise, was the power of the past over the German imagination. 'The Teuton has a thorough knowledge of his craft, his technical skill is unlimited, but he lacks freshness of inspiration; . . . Every production of art throughout the world, from the earliest times, is known to the Germans, and remembered too, for they assimilate easily, and have great receptive qualities. But how rare it is to find in their work a really novel aspect of things, anything showing that it has sprung spontaneously from the heart and the hand, from the very innermost being of the artist or the craftsman.'

Of the exhibits on which Mourey commented in detail, Bruno Paul's 'Hunting Room' was adjudged 'the best, because it is the most simple and the most harmonious, production . . .' and Max Läuger's ceramic work was also considered successful. Bernhard Pankok's room was 'somewhat sombre', an impression reinforced by that of Richard Riemerschmid's room where a 'sense of depression' was generated: 'the style is gloomy and austere – almost sepulchural.' In contrast great enthusiasm was expressed for the work of the Darmstadt colony, where 'everything is bright and joyous, full of happy fancy and true elegance.' [92] Many of Mourey's detailed comments were apposite and justified, but in his general observations and conclusions he demonstrated that nationalist prejudice and bias were not the sole perquisites of German critics.

Although, as Paris clearly demonstrated, the old guard of academic practitioners was still to be reckoned with, a dramatic contrast was evident in the next important event outside Germany. The International Exhibition of Applied Art in Turin of 1902 was organized by several applied art organizations, though with government subsidy, through a committee chaired by Hans von Berlepsch, who was also responsible for the exhibition building. Peter Behrens' entrance hall, commissioned by the Hamburg Museum of Applied Art, aroused considerable comment. It was a total concept, spacious yet intimate in scale, a composition of restrained curvilinear forms. The detailed execution was by a group of Hamburg's leading craftsmen, utilizing some unusual materials, aluminium, leather and cane. Decorative effect was achieved by highlighting structures rather than applying extraneous effects, and a profusion of hanging plants provided a soft counterpoint to the man-made forms. With hindsight, it can be seen as one of the final expressions of *Jugendstil* by Behrens, who even then was exploring new directions. In its time and context, however, it appeared strikingly innovative, earning widespread approval, with one critic, Georg Fuchs, suggesting it was

Tiled wall-fountain by Max Läuger exhibited in the German pavilion, 1900 Paris Exposition.

Portal of the German pavilion at the International Exhibition of Applied Art in Turin, 1902, designed by Hans von Berlepsch.

Entrance hall to the German pavilion, Turin, 1902, designed by Peter Behrens in association with a group of Hamburg artists and craftsmen.

A bedroom, one of a suite of three rooms exhibited by J-M Olbrich at the 1902 Turin exhibition which were accorded widespread and lavish praise.

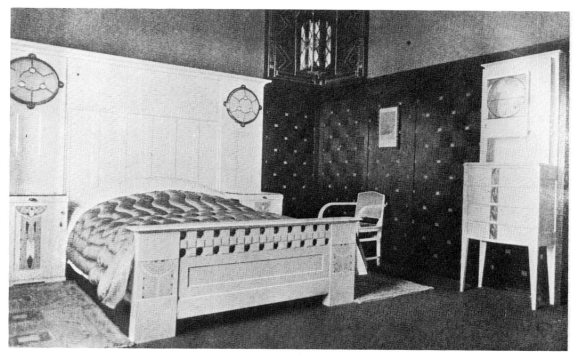

perhaps the first synthesis of Germany's lines of inner and outer power. In an article remarkable for its ecstatic chauvinism and breathtakingly florid prose, he designated it 'The House of Might and Beauty', and proclaimed: '"Enter stranger, here the German Reich holds sway; see with joyful heart of what it is capable!" – A sentence of this kind should be carved over the entrance-arch. For what the silent voices make known in this hall, is might, the might of the Reich of Wilhelm II, ready, prepared and determined, equally entitled, equally endowed amongst the world powers to assert its place in the new division of the globe, which the destiny of nations has declared as its immutable decree.' [93]

Behrens also designed a library-room commissioned by Alexander Koch, but generally the greatest praise was for three rooms by Olbricht, The Studio considering him 'almost a classic master' [94]. Apart from the Darmstadt influence, however, artists from other centres and firms associated with the

applied art movement also exhibited, for example, Karl Gross, Wilhelm Kreis and the Kleinhempels from Dresden; almost inevitably, the Vereinigte Werkstätten; Kayser, and Villeroy & Boch, amongst many others. As a whole it was very well received and secured further international recognition for the scale and significance of developments in Germany.

The momentum was further maintained two years on, in 1904, at the St Louis Exposition in the USA, this time organized by state commissioners. Maude Oliver reported in The Studio, 'according to the verdict of their best critics, the German work seen at Turin, which had previously been unprecedented, was mediocre as compared with the St Louis showing, both in the matter of excellence and of effect.' She was obviously impressed herself, to judge by the number of superlatives in her article, commenting on the general impression: 'The beautiful and the useful are so united in sentiment and in substance, as to yield an equilibrium of repose.' [95]

Alexander Koch was so excited by the positive reaction that an article in *Deutsche Kunst und Dekoraten* was hurriedly advanced a month, and readers could hardly have been disappointed by it. The report, by Hermann Muthesius, said the German exhibits put those of other lands into the shade. 'Many of its achievements are so pure and stand on such an inassailable artistic height, that even the enemies of everything modern must lower their sails.' That mixture of metaphors was followed by the assertion: 'Germany has achieved a total indisputable applied art victory. Indeed, the German applied art presentation must necessarily arouse the idea in every visitor, that today the centre of applied art development lies in Germany, perhaps in the same measure, as it lay in France from the time of Louis XIV onward.'[96]

The array of talent represented in the German applied art section was most certainly impressive, a roll call of the best talent in the country, with all the familiar names and organizations represented, and what was particularly important, there was strength in depth, with many artists who were less familiar to an international audience making a considerable impact, such as Adalbert Niemayer and Karl Bertsch of the *Münchner Werkstätten für Wohnungseinrichtungen,* which they had founded in 1902; Anton Huber of Berlin, whose dining room was thought by Maude Oliver to be 'particularly pleasing'; and a group from Magdeburg led by Albin Müller who presented a room, of which Theodor Volbehr commented: 'The content, moulded in such taut, clear, logical forms, is pronouncedly German. Not only because in it German materials have everywhere been utilized, but because everything is created with an intimate sense for the still poetry of the home.'[97] Also, for the first time, the exhibition commission saw fit to allocate a room to the *Verein der Kunstlerinnen und Kunstfreundinnen* (Association of Women Artists and Art Lovers), which was of a high standard, though generally felt to be suffering from an attempt to include the diverse work of too many contributors. Across the whole range exhibited, there were fewer signs of the influence of *Jugendstil,* the prevailing note being of clearly articulated forms, emphasizing the quality of materials in a subtle and harmonious manner.

The St Louis Exposition was undoubtedly a crucial event for the reform movement, which had there gained representation under state auspices on such a large scale and had justified it with an outstanding success. Above all, from that time forward, a new note of confidence became apparent that encouraged further effort and achievement. There were many other similar international events in subsequent years, but none had quite the impact of St Louis.

If government support for international exhibitions had paid off handsomely, there were also considerable advances under the aegis of the various state governments, particularly in education. In Prussia, for example, considerable influence was exercised by Hermann Muthesius.

An architect by training, Muthesius had visited Japan as a student, after which he joined the Prussian Civil Service. In 1896 he was posted to the German Embassy in London as architectural attaché, to observe trends in British architecture and design relevant to German developments. The suggestion for such an appointment apparently stemmed from the Emperor, and was a clear indication of the importance attached to art and design in the national image. During his time in London, Muthesius became enthused by the Arts and Crafts movement, cultivating close relationships with many leading practitioners. In addition to official reports, a wider public was informed of his impressions through books and frequent articles. Returning to Germany in 1903 he was appointed to the Prussian Ministry of Trade and Commerce with responsibility for art education and embarked on reform based on his observ-

Ante-room to the dining room designed by Anton Huber for the German applied art pavilion at the 1904 St Louis Exposition in the USA.

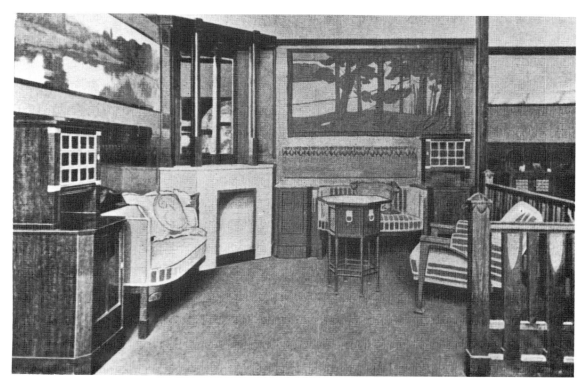

Collective exhibit by the Association of Women Artists and Art Lovers for the German pavilion at the 1904 St Louis Exposition.

Two plates painted by
Leonhard Hellmuth in
1866 demonstrate the
growing interest in flat,
natural patterns rather
than historical revivalism
at this time.

Salon writing desk with
chair designed in 1883
by the architect and
sculptor Adolf
Guggenberger and
executed by the court
gilder A. Pütterich of
Munich. The encrusted
form and costly materials
are typical of the more
extreme manifestations
of Rococo style in
southern Germany.

The penchant for decorative and symbolic form in the late nineteenth century is also evident in this cast-iron post box of the Royal Bavarian Post c.1890. The front panel juxtaposes information on collection times with the royal coat-of-arms and Renaissance decoration. The essential function of posting letters is relegated to a side panel.
(Verkehrsmuseum, Nuremburg)

Sideboard designed by Henry van der Velde and produced in solid mahogany with brass fittings by his own workshops near Brussels in 1898. The design is unusual for its height, the combination of side and bottom-hinged doors, and the cantilevered surface.
(Kunsthandwerks-museum Frankfurt/Main)

A dish and range of majolica vases by Max Läuger of Karlsruhe illustrated in *Deutsche Kunst und Dekoration* in 1897, which clearly demonstrates his virtuosity in exploiting natural decorative motifs which were an integral element of his forms. The limitations of contemporary photographic printing do little justice however to his vivid, iridescent colours.

The St George Chest
c.1890, made in the
Rhineland, designer
unknown, was an
attempt to re-interpret
Gothic values in
contemporary form.
(Museum für Kunst und
Gewerbe, Hamburg)

A pair of water jugs and wash bowls in stoneware produced in Sarreguemines c.1900, designer unknown. The abstracted lemon fruit and leaf decor illustrates the extent to which concepts of natural form allied to simple basic shapes had replaced historical decoration in everyday wares by the turn of the century. (Stadtmuseum, Munich)

Bed designed by Henry van der Velde for Otto Meier of Munich c.1898. This piece in solid walnut was another example of the individual pieces produced in the Uccle workshops shortly before van der Velde left for Germany. (Stadtmuseum, Munich)

ations of English practice.

Shortly after his appointment, Muthesius was the responsible official behind a ministerial decree which introduced workshop training in the crafts into Prussian schools of applied art. It was intended 'to emphatically give the student an awareness of the necessary relationship between raw materials and form and to educate him to develop his design more objectively, more economically and more functionally. Through engagement with materials the student will further eliminate misguided concepts, such as that the production of superficially pleasing drawings would be a worthwhile purpose, without concern for whether they paid adequate attention to the materials and its qualities. Also purely artistically, the workshops can only enable valuable stimulation, which instead of superficial accepted forms, is founded on the insight into constructional possibilities (Gestaltungs-Möglichkeiten) won through their own activity.' [98] The intention, therefore, was to end the emphasis on drawing detached from an understanding of materials, and the initiative was intended to be valid both for crafts and industry. It was seen by one commentator, at least, as a precondition for closer links between art and industry to the benefit of both: 'With the current application of new materials and taking into account the chemical and physical knowledge of our age, such a unification of theory and practice is essential to artistic and economic progress.' [99]

Muthesius used his patronage in appointments to directorships of schools to further this policy. In this and other activities he exemplified the considerable influence civil servants were capable of exercising in Germany. One of the first appointments in 1903, was of Peter Behrens as director of the Düsseldorf school, where he introduced sweeping reforms. His first programme stated: 'The Applied Arts School pursues the aim of training qualified workers for the requirements of applied arts and art industry and to have a generally stimulating and supportive influence on domestic applied art. This will be achieved through systematic education of the students to good taste and to a feeling for the organic in structure and arrangement, through instruction of the student in graphic and plastic representation, through close connection with the crafts and research into the means of construction and structure of materials, through education to artistic self-sufficiency and independence.' [100] The Vorschule (Preliminary School) of two years duration was the foundation of his teaching programme, in which general courses, nature studies and free-drawing were combined with technical construction exercises, technical drawing, letter-forms and workshop instruction. Five professional classes: architecture, sculpture, surface and graphic art, decorative painting and engraving, were subsequently available. These were all workshop based, to give a command of materials and technique.

Also in 1903, Hans Poelzig was appointed Director of the Royal School of Arts and Crafts at Breslau, though by the Prussian Ministry of Education under whose competence the school lay. There, he developed a curriculum emphasizing craft education as not simply a familiarization with technique but as an instrument for developing ethical values in students.

In 1907, at the instigation of Wilhelm von Bode, director of the Berlin Museum, Bruno Paul was invited to head the school attached to it. The need, according to Bode, was for someone to bring clear leadership to the institution. 'Our choice fell on Paul who had already mostly laid aside the bad habits of the Jugendstil and appeared to us to most originally link-up with older models.' [101] Bode feared the Emperor would veto the appointment, for Paul had earlier contributed many drawings to Simplicissimus, often satirizing the monarch and his government, but it was, despite that, approved.

Paul, too, firmly believed in the workshop tradition of instruction and sought to re-establish its relevance. He introduced a dual system of instruction in basic courses, with *Werkmeister* (foremen) responsible for the craft side, alongside technically trained teachers responsible for artistic training. After passing a test, students were eligible for admission to a subject class, one of a large range of specialisms under a Professor. There, the work demands were increased but more was left to students' own initiative. Specially gifted students could later become assistants for up to six years, giving them an opportunity to develop their own work and earn a living, whilst the school had the stimulus of fresh, youthful ideas.

Another appointment of great significance, this time in Saxony, was of Henry van der Velde to Weimar. He was initially invited in 1902 by the Grand Duke of Saxe-Weimar to act as 'artistic counsellor charged with restoring the aesthetic level of all the craft and industrial production of the region.' That wording was deceptive; in fact his role was to help the crafts and small producers in the struggle to survive the competition of big industrial units. At Weimar, he initiated an 'Applied Arts Seminar' for young workers in employment. The concept was for students or apprentices to bring materials for a task of current relevance from their workplace, specifically commissioned by their master craftsman. Under the guidance of teachers at the seminar they would work towards a finished model to be taken back to the workplace and put into production. It was therefore intended to have an applied research function of immediate relevance and benefit to small producers. Van der Velde hoped the reliance on them for materials and tasks would eliminate the need for separate research workshops, and would help overcome any mistrust of the seminar as a threat. At the same time, work was underway on buildings for a Grand Ducal School of Applied Arts, to van der Velde's designs, which opened in 1906, with himself as principal. In the next few years he committed considerable energy to establishing contacts and good relationships with local small industry, for whom the courses at the school were intended, though with only limited success.

Thus in the first decade of the new century a significant challenge to the traditions of formal academic instruction emerged in Germany with widespread official support. Supporters of the old system could, however, also point to its successes. In 1909, an exhibition was held to celebrate the 45th anniversary of the Munich School of Applied Art. To comprehend this event, *The Studio* wrote, it must be borne in mind that it was organized 'by a single city with a population of little more than half a million.'[102] An article on French design in this period records a similar comment from *Le Figaro*, 'Here is a city of 500,000 inhabitants that, with its own resources, organizes a strictly local exhibition and manages to fill six large halls and four hundred rooms with the products of its own activity alone. I look in vain for another city where a work of such magnitude could have been produced.'[103] Another French visitor confessed his amazement at the progress evident in Munich. 'All these observations caused our surprise, but this was transformed into stupefaction when we saw the work exhibited by the Munich professional schools, from the elementary to the advanced level... As for the objects exhibited by the students of the College of Decorative Arts, they would be worthy of inclusion in our museums!'[104] Such praise from a Frenchman must have been music to the ears of any German who might have read it, but it was a serious indication of how fast Germany was progressing and of the contribution made by the education system at all levels.

The number of different agencies at all levels of government, and local and regional

Hall in the 'Old Munich' style designed by Gabriel von Seidl for the Munich Exhibition of Decorative Arts, 1908, an example of the penchant for nostalgia that still existed in Germany despite the efforts of reformers.

variations make it difficult to generalize about the influence of such bodies. They could just as easily champion conservative or restorationist values. In 1901, Karl Schmidt was involved with the *Verein für sächsische Volkskunde* (Society for Saxon Folklore), which persuaded the Royal Saxon Ministry of the Interior to cooperate in a joint venture to encourage an awareness of traditional values and the protection of the environment. The Ministry directed all heads of architectural, applied art and technical schools to make pupils aware of local and traditional forms and to collect sketches of valuable examples to be shown in a public exhibition. Schmidt wrote of this exercise: 'We still stand under the influence of the speech given in Bonn by the Emperor, in which he — finding the most fortunate expression for the inner feelings of our nation — referred to the necessity of our development in a national German sense. And indeed architecture, as the most fundamental of all arts, requires such a development, such a

Kitchen designed by Otto Bauer for the Munich Exhibition of 1908. Although little attention was yet being given to the efficiency of kitchen lay-outs, this design was an effort to create a bright and pleasant working environment.

requirement of the sense of German unique-ness, if the last remnant of German uniqueness and with it all that which is of value and irreplaceable in our inner and national life is not to be wholly lost. Should our Germany remain in the possession of the Germanic race, so it also needs in our architecture the resumption and more powerful emphasis of German nature. The understanding for this can, however, only be awakened, preserved and empowered if the works of our forebears find more appreciation, if everything foreign is held distant from the crystallization process and simply, or rather predominantly, the national element is emphasized.' [105] Such views explain why Schmidt later became a founder-member and leading activist in the Saxon *Heimatschutz*.

The Royal Saxon Ministry of the Interior also became involved in other, related, activities to help the crafts, for instance, commissioning an investigation and calling a conference in 1906 to inquire into whether traditional crafts were being seriously disadvantaged by new art tendencies. The result was recommen-dations to restrict the exhibition of novelties, and discussions between craft organizations and the Leipzig Museum of Applied Art and its *Kunstgewerbeverein* to effect positive initiatives. [106]

A further aspect of government influence was the possibility of exercising direct patronage through purchases and public commissions. The earliest government agency to bestow its patronage on the new applied art was, somewhat surprisingly, the Imperial German Navy. In an article published in 1907, Wilhelm Scholermann described a visit to the armoured cruiser *Fürst Bismarck,* some eight years earlier, recalling the clash be-tween exterior and interior design. In 1905 he wrote, invited on a short voyage in a torpedo-boat, this impression was revived. Of the outer lines and the mechanisms: 'Certainly there lay in them a new beauty.' In contrast, however, the officers' quarters, in late Renaissance and early Baroque style, stood 'in contradiction to the spirit and ideas of the present . . . Old and new complement each other quite well sometimes. But not bad stylistic imitation with the living spirit of modern technology.' Scholermann was of the opinion that artists needed to learn from engineers, many of whom had an instinct for form and style. [107]

These views were a reiteration of ideas widespread at this time, and it seems curious that Scholermann was unaware of recent events. In 1903, Karl Schmidt decided the *Dresdener Werkstätten* ought to become in-volved in producing ships-fittings and visited Hamburg and Kiel to explore the possibilities of business. Interestingly, his conservationist convictions did not in any respect conflict with his highly successful entrepreneurial career. According to his own account, he managed to get an interview in Kiel with a shipyard director, Dr Rossfeld, who on brusquely de-manding Schmidt's purpose, was asked to listen to the latter for three minutes. The reply was an abrupt affirmative. Said Schmidt: 'If you build ships, you take the best engineers and constructors, and that is right. If you fit out ships, you take any kind of furnishings, and that is not right.' Rossfeld became interested and was persuaded to allow Richard Riemer-schmid to prepare some designs. On return-ing with plans and costings, Schmidt was met by the Admiral in charge of naval construction at Kiel and a team of directors and naval architects from the shipyard. Emphasis has rightly been placed on Schmidt's artistic and social idealism in many descriptions of him, but he must also have been a superb sales-man. Not only did he secure acceptance for Riemerschmid's designs, which was not too difficult since they were enthusiastically received, but he convinced the shipyard team to alter the internal configuration of a vessel to allow the designs to be fully realized. [108] As a further indication of his success, in the following decade, commissions to equip the

Richard Riemerschmid's design for the officers' mess of the light cruiser SMS *Danzig*, 1905, executed by the Dresdener Werkstätten, Hellerau.

The captain's quarters of the light cruiser SMS *Danzig* designed in 1905 by Richard Riemerschmid for the Dresdener Werkstätten, Hellerau.

Columnar supports and railings designed for overhead sections of the Berlin Electric Railway. A section for the station at Bulowstrasse by Bruno Mohring.

Interior of the Danzigerstrasse station of the Berlin electric railway by Alfred Grenander. This was a later design by Grenander for the system and indicates the extent to which his concepts had become simplified.

Second class railcar interior the Berlin electric railway, designed by Alfred Grenander c.1910

Station entrance to the Berlin electric railway at Wittenberg Platz by Alfred Grenander, c.1901. *Jugendstil* influences are very evident in the ironwork patterns of the entrance and railings.

captains' cabins and officers' messes of thirteen naval vessels, beginning with the armoured cruiser *Prinz Adalbert* and the light cruisers *Berlin* and *Danzig* in the period 1904-06, were received. The limited spatial dimensions called for great economy of means, with storage in box-forms tucked into niches and running along walls, enabling the maximum space allowable within available limits to be used to create a pleasant, relaxing atmosphere.

The patronage of *land* and city authorities could also be substantial. For example, in 1898 the first stages of construction began on a new electric overhead and underground railway system commissioned by the Berlin municipality. It provoked considerable debate on the need to take into account the effect of such major construction on the capital's street image. *Deutsche Bauzeitung* published a series of eight articles on the project by Albert Hoffmann, in which the purely functional approach adopted in similar projects in America and Britain were cited as an indication of the materialism prevalent in those countries. In contrast, German aspirations were to achieve pure beauty in construction which required a measure of 'aesthetic superfluity' and Hoffmann specifically rejected the proposition that 'functionality is beauty.' [109]

Four architects, Sepp Kaiser, Alfred Grenander, Bruno Mohring and Stadtbaurat Jautschuss were commissioned for work on the Berlin project under the consulting architect, Paul Wittig. Initially, they produced designs of a decorative nature for station street entrances and columnar supports for the overhead sections, but both city council and public were very concerned at the image of the railway, and work later broadened, with, for example, Alfred Grenander becoming responsible for designing stations, service buildings and rolling stock for the system up until 1914. Prior to 1897, Grenander had worked for seven years under the architect Wallot on the Reichstag building. In this work, however, he evolved clean, functional and well-detailed forms of a high standard. In moving away from applied decoration, he translated the concept of 'aesthetic superfluity' into something more subtle, a concern for form in relation to function, though not determined by it. Of his work as a whole, a critic commented: 'Practicality in the garment of taste is Grenander's ideal. He therefore cultivates straightness and parallelism. His ceilings and walls, his furniture and lighting apparatus, are treated with some of the soberness of the engineer. Yet the aesthetic is also active in him, and asserts itself in softening and embellishing; vertical lines are therefore sometimes gently inclined, and strong colours tempered. The logician cannot resist the temptation of the graces.' [110]

If Grenander's designs for the Berlin transport network were in the context of a major public work, it is also worth noting that it would have been impossible without the support of the contractors for the project, Siemens Halske. Their role was recognized when the Rector and Senate of Berlin's Technical University unanimously approved the award of an honorary doctorate in 1906 to the retiring chief architect of Siemens, Heinrich Schwieger, for his contributions to the development of the city's transport system. Siemens had close links and worked in close co-operation with official bodies at all levels, like most large German companies. However, by the turn of the century these were developing an influence on design in their own right, offering a wide range of commissions that were often substantial in scope.

8 Developments in German Industry

The structure of German industry was variegated: at its peak were large combines of a size and complexity unmatched in Europe, such as Krupp or Thyssen which dominated basic industries, bringing together coal, steel and heavy engineering in a co-ordinated production sequence, and new giant companies in more recently developed areas of production, such as the electrical industry and chemicals. In trading too, shipping lines such as North German Lloyd and Hamburg-Amerika held a powerful position due to their scale and capitalization, and in the retail sector there was a marked growth of large department stores.

A contemporary English observer wrote of this concentration: 'Perhaps no specially German characteristic has proved of greater service in the struggle for commercial and industrial mastery than the faculty for organization and co-operation. Individualism is good where it has free play, but under modern industrial conditions pure individualism is inadequate, and even were it not inadequate it is impracticable in many large spheres of private enterprise. The most striking expression of this instinct for organization is seen in the remarkable growth of large undertakings. . . Against the old political maxim "Divide and rule", the modern Caesars of industry and commerce advance the principle "Unite and conquer". . . The union now in favour may take various forms — a loose convention, a close combination, or a formal fusion or amalgamation — but whatever the form the ends sought and, in fact, attained, are the elimination of competition and greater economy in working.'[111]

The largest firms had grown by directly taking over rival concerns, but in manufacturing, cartels and syndicates were widespread. Cartels were a looser form of organization, directed to securing an equalization of conditions of sale, usually in the form of price-fixing, but sometimes extending to an allocation of particular spheres of production or markets. Syndicates were more tightly structured, taking over marketing, pricing and general policy, and leaving only internal organization, and decisions on the nature and quality of the goods produced to individual firms. 'In that form they may be described as Socialistic organizations working for individualistic ends.'[112] In the latter context it was estimated that real power and control in German industry rested with some three hundred individuals.

Under these circumstances there were several implications for design. If the director of a large undertaking could be convinced of the significance of visual form in terms of commercial efficiency and image, there was a possibility of making rapid progress in furthering the ends of cultural reform, as in the case of Karl Schmidt gaining contracts for naval vessels. Secondly, the elimination of direct price competition in many industries and markets led to an emphasis on other factors, such as product identity and quality, in which design could be a vital factor. Finally, in more general terms, there was, at some levels of German management, a belief in the vital cultural role of industry in contemporary society, which inclined them to take arguments on the potential social significance of visual form more seriously than was commonly the case in other countries. Although self-interest undoubtedly lay behind such attitudes, this was not felt to conflict with a sense of social responsibility, rather the two were mutually reinforcing.

In addition to the giants of German industry, however, there were in the middle range many firms in which traditional methods had

Kitchen scales by Robert Krups of Soling with Majoloca housing. This design was one of many for this type of domestic appliance, many of which were only superficially different, which were produced in-house by Krups' staff in the years before the First World War.

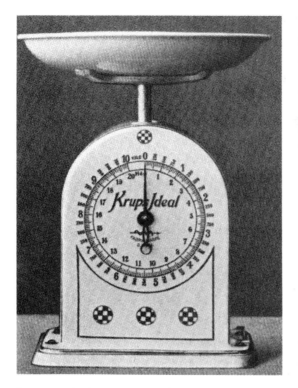

been scaled-up to meet larger markets, and also more recently founded companies exploiting new technologies for new products in the growing consumer market, such as W.M.F. or Krups. Finally there was a large number of small craft or artisan businesses of all kinds that suffered varying fortunes, some adapting and enjoying a modest prosperity, others hit hard by mass-production competitors.

The pace and effect of industrialization since unification had left traditional modes of production at a severe disadvantage, and needs also to be taken into account in understanding the reaction in design theory and many organizations to the effects of modernization, which can be illustrated by some basic statistics. The population of Germany increased from 41 million in 1870 to 65 million in 1910, but the bulk of the growth swelled the

larger cities. In 1871 there were eight large cities (classed as over 100,000 inhabitants), which grew to 43 in number by 1910, their inhabitants comprising almost 5% of the population in 1871 and over 21% in 1910. The urban population as a percentage of the national total similarly grew in the same period from 36% to 60%. A corresponding decrease in relative terms was evident in the figures for rural communes. Whilst their total population over this period shows a very slight decrease of a quarter of a million people, the proportion of rural dwellers in the population as a whole fell from 64% in 1871 to 40% in 1910. [113]

Within those figures lay a substantial swing towards a population increasingly dependent upon industrial production in an urban environment, which many saw as a threat to the inherited patterns of life, and which accounts

The first prize award in a competition for workers' furnishings organized by Krupp of Essen in 1901, went to this design by H.E. Mieritz of Berlin. Detailed designs for all the furniture were also provided, it was of sound construction based on plain, rural models.

for the frequently repeated calls for protection and aid to mitigate the continual erosion of rural crafts. Many of the latter were dependent upon domestic work, where conditions were often appalling. The toy industry which had been a staple of many rural communities, for example, was particularly affected by mechanization. The work was hard and monotonous, for although hand work was the norm, there was also a high degree of division of labour between households. 'Representatives of the toy industry of the Ore Mountains present at the Berlin Congress of Home Workers of 1911 instanced wages of 8s.6d. a week for an entire family working fourteen and fifteen hours a day.' [114] The terrible conditions of the domestic textiles industry of Silesia had earlier been vividly portrayed in Gerhardt Hauptmann's play 'The Weavers'. If nostalgia for a lost past was at the heart of many calls for a revitalization of the crafts, the misery of domestic workers as a consequence of mechanization provided the impetus for other political and economic initiatives, although the former rather than the latter found expression in the cultural reform movement, which generally focussed either on the possibilities of influencing industry or of establishing the newer form of craft workshop.

Industry was not simply the pawn of cultural reformers, however, but also initiated programmes arising from a perception of its own needs and interests. In this, the paternalistic tendency of German society was often apparent. Krupp, for example, provided a range of welfare and recreational services for its employees within a regimen demanding loyalty and discipline. In the early twentieth century the number of direct employees of Krupp was estimated at 70,000, and in order to attract skilled workers and maintain their loyalty, the company had long been involved in the provision of housing, which was further extended to a concern for the contents of workers' dwellings. In 1901, in co-operation with a Düsseldorf housing association, Krupp

organized a competition for furnishings in working-class housing, with a brief specifying '. . . domestic fittings, which without all unnecessary ornament and without imitating fine types of timber, are comfortable, functional and beautiful, and yet do not require more means for purchase than those previously available.' [115] The designs were to be for a living-kitchen, living-room and bedroom. To dissuade workers from 'the many poor products presently on the market', a very tight cost ceiling was imposed. The winner out of 122 entries was a Berlin architect, H.E. Mieritz, whose designs were solid, simplified forms of rustic models. The appropriateness of such country forms for industrial workers is, in retrospect, questionable, though the concept of emphasizing roots in the land for alienated city dwellers was widespread at the time. The views of workers on the prize-winning entries is unknown, for they were not consulted, and it would have been highly unusual had that been the case. The designs were, in fact, an idealized image of what workers ought to want, rather than what they desired, ignoring a tendency for them to purchase decorative products for their homes as a surrogate for aspirations to status denied them in other aspects of their lives.

A more direct and widespread influence

An electric kitchen illustrated in *Innen-Dekoration* in 1896, executed by P. Stotz of Stuttgart. The display cases on the right and sign in the centre indicate that this was a demonstration room for exhibition purposes. (courtesy: RIBA)

Advertisement for the Berlin lighting equipment firm of C. Niemann & Co., 1906, which both in text and image stresses that decorative concerns were to the fore in its appeal to customers.

Although attention has focussed predominantly on the two giant companies of the German electrical industry, AEG and Siemens, many others, often of considerable size, were active in this field. Amongst the best known was the Frankfurt company, Prometheus, which manufactured a wide range of appliances, generally of clean unadorned appearance.

stemmed from a wholly new range of consumer products which flowed from factories in even larger quantities, as in the electrical industry. This was dominated by two giants, Siemens and the *Allgemeine Elektrizitäts Gesellschaft* (AEG), each having a huge product range from complete power-stations to small domestic appliances. Expanding generating capacity was a great stimulus to their continuing growth, electricity stations increasing from 148 in 1894 to 1028 in 1904, though whilst lighting capacity increased four-fold, that for power leapt over twenty-fold. [116] Powered appliances for workplace and home therefore came to occupy a large role in expanding production, with, for example, AEG's turnover increasing by 20% in 1906-07. [117]

The growth in exports by such companies

was also considerable, and aroused considerable comment overseas, for example, in some categories doubling in the twelve months between 1906-07. [118] Increases of this scale were achieved by a vigorous effort on the part of firms, supported by the Imperial Government. An English electrical journal noted in 1907 that commercial attachés were being appointed to German consulates: 'It is the duty of these commercial attachés to increase Germany's foreign trade, and these experts of trade and commerce are always in direct communication with all the leading manufacturing and exporting houses of the German Empire, and make frequent trips to Germany for the purpose of personal conference with them.' [119] Such a level of organization and initiative was eventually be extended to the function of design in many companies.

Product forms were generally designed in-house by engineers or model-makers, those for industrial use being starkly functional, whilst those for domestic purposes had added decoration intended to satisfy prevailing tastes. A stronger consciousness of aesthetic imagery was apparent in company buildings and exhibitions, of which Siemens organized thirty across Europe in 1902, and in advertising. AEG employed well-known architects to design office blocks and artists for posters, catalogues and brochures, a task Otto Eckmann performed for the company's presentation at the 1900 Paris Exposition. The forms and imagery applied frequently bore little relationship, however, to the nature of the firms and their technology, with symbolic figures from Classical and Germanic mythology being predominant.

In the middle range of companies producing goods having a long tradition, furniture, ceramics, glass and metalware, no one identifiable pattern was evident. Many companies employed a staff of draughtsmen and modellers, however, there were constraints and problems influencing the introduction of new

forms. When Schneider and Hanau of Frankfurt/Main, a leading 'art-furniture' manufacturer, introduced a new range 'in the modern style' in 1898, designed in-house by their own employees, it was recognized 'that a large factory can obviously not advance so radically with a new character as a single artist, but more slowly since it must lead and educate its personnel as well as its customers.' The new range of the company was attributed to 'the artistic seriousness and understanding of the director' supported by an 'extraordinarily well-trained staff of designers, wood-carvers, cabinet-makers and mechanics.' [120] An effective lead from management, the requisite skill and talent amongst the design staff, and an awareness of what the market is capable of being led to, rather than simply what it is believed it will accept, remains a combination that promotes successful design policy in business to this day.

Where companies employed artists for occasional consultancy, the list often included distinguished names. In the early years of the century in the Rhineland-Westphalia region, the Rheinische Glashütten AG employed Peter Behrens, J.V. Cissarz, Kolo Moser, Joseph Olbrich and Erich Kleinhempel; the Metalwarenfabrik Gerhardi Cie from 1902 had Behrens and Olbrich, Maurice Dufréne, Paul Haustein, Albin Müller and Albert Reimann; and at the same time Behrens, Olbrich and Müller also worked for a neighbouring firm of Hueck. [121] The cachet of attaching the names of well-known artists to products, particularly if prefixed by the academic title of 'Professor', was a desirable status symbol for many producers. Their designs were for luxury products, however, having no relationship to the general production runs, and there were reported functional problems due to artists pushing materials beyond acceptable limits.

The advocacy of a unified formal aesthetic which stressed simplification could, in fact, ignore the real problems of processing some

'Large lounge in modern character', one of a series of drawings to illustrate the new furniture range produced by the Frankfurt firm of Schneider and Hanau in 1898. (courtesy: RIBA)

A set of table glasses
with red feet designed by
Peter Behrens for the
Rheinische Glashütten in
1901. Such 'artistic'
designs were the
exception in most
companies output.

Two cast iron domestic
heating 'modern stoves'
designed by J-M Olbrich
in 1901 for Oscar Winter
of Hannover.

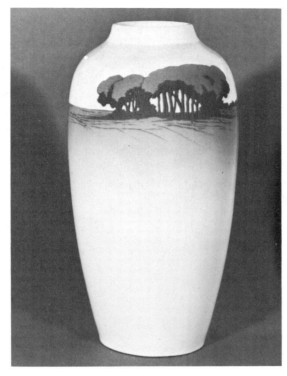

A 1907 advertisement for the Hannover iron-founders, Oscar Winter, who specialized in cooking and heating appliances.

Theo Schmuz-Baudiss, vase for the Royal Porcelain Manufactory, Berlin, 1903. (courtesy: Badisches Landesmuseum, Karlsruhe)

Cup and saucer for the Royal Porcelain Manufactory, Berlin by Theo Schmuz-Baudiss, 1901. (courtesy: Badisches Landesmuseum, Karlsruhe)

materials. In the working of sheet-metal, for example, structure and simplicity could be easily emphasized since the surface of the material was smooth and clean, requiring relatively little finishing. Moulded wares, however, still used reliefs, because technically it was difficult to achieve smooth surfaces — they required more work and were thus more difficult. This was particularly the case if small, unavoidable moulding defects came too clearly to light.

A similar pattern was evident in the ceramics industry, which had well-established staffs of designers and modellers trained in-house, but which also recognized the need for new ideas to keep pace with market changes. The Royal Berlin Porcelain Manufactory appointed the painter Theo Schmuz-Baudiss, who had developed a highly individual approach to ceramics, as artistic designer in 1903, in order to develop modern forms whilst at the same time, continuing to evolve its

traditional techniques and designs. 'Sudden changes have been cleverly avoided, and yet modernism has found a widely-opened entrance.' [122]

The problems of change were not always easily resolved, however, as was the case with one of the most illustrious names in German ceramics: the Royal Saxon Manufactory at Meissen, whose products had market difficulties owing to it resting on past laurels and not adapting to changes in taste. 'It is naturally much easier to establish the fact that there is something wrong,' wrote Professor H.W. Singer 'than to point out exactly the remedy. There is evidently need of an artist at the head of the factory, which has for years been virtually run by businessmen.' [123] If some companies had enlightened managers, Meissen obviously did not and suffered a disadvantage as a result. The greatest difficulties identified by Singer were in introducing modern work. Some artists had been

Part of the workshops at the Royal Saxon Porcelain Manufactory, Meissen, c.1890. Production was still by individual potters repetitively throwing the same piece and there are few signs of modern processes or organization.

appointed to life positions and others were used as outside consultants to furnish models, but the experience did not seem to be a happy one. 'Van der Velde sent in a design for a coffee-set. When executed it proved to be not at all charming, but rather clumsy. His dinner-set shows better shapes. But like everything that this artist has done, it is all van der Velde, and not a bit porcelain . . . The design is in no way adapted to the material, it would do as well for a book-cover, or a title-page, or a piece of furniture. Richard Riemerschmid has also furnished a dinner-set with a simple non-realistic linear decoration in cobalt-blue. The ornamentation is not bad, but there is nothing overwhelming about it.' [124]

However, alongside the production of traditional goods, frequently still dependent on craft methods, were other firms utilizing new materials such as Britannia metal and aluminium and techniques of enamelling metal pressings, to produce domestic goods in large quantities. Despite dominating the popular market their products were rarely considered in art journals, but although their internal structure is unclear, there seems to have been attempts at 'styling' by companies such as Krups of Solingen and Henschels Zwillingswerke [125]. As had been realized by many companies in Britain and the United States in the nineteenth century, the cost of decoration in terms of design time, patterns and moulds was a minimal proportion of overall production costs, but could significantly improve market image and sales value.

Research on this period has tended to concentrate on varied aspects of the cultural reform movement and, furthermore, has overwhelmingly reflected its point of view and values. It can therefore be difficult to assess what impact it had on general patterns of production, taste and consumption.

An example of trends in a wider context is the 1912 catalogue of a mail-order company, August Stukenbrok of Einbeck, near Göttingen. [126] The company, named after its

Wall fountain in stoneware with decorative mountings in Orivit pewter by the Cologne firm of F.H.Schmitz c.1899. In such a piece, the dividing line between the naturalism of the 1880s and early *Jugendstil* becomes indistinct and difficult to discern. (Museum für Kunst und Gewerbe, Hamburg)

Ceiling light in opalescent glass for Peter Behrens' Hamburg hall in the German pavilion at the Turin Exhibition of 1902. Behrens' work at this exhibition marked a turning away from curvilinear early *Jugendstil* to more regular, geometric forms, though the transition, as evident in this pattern, is not entirely complete.

Poster by Otto Fischer for an exhibition of Saxon Crafts and Applied Art in Dresden, 1896. Its imagery of traditional dress and architecture contrasted strongly with the assured competence shown in exploiting the potential of modern lithographic processing, typical of the German printing industry at that time.

Part of a dining room set designed by Bernhard Pankok in 1898-9 for the Vereinigte Werkstätten in Munich. The timber was dark stained Danube oak and the curving forms are typical of the early *Jugendstil* products of this workshop. (Kunsthandwerksmuseum, Frankfurt/Main)

The official poster by Otto Gussman for the Third German Applied Art Exhibition held at Dresden in 1906.

Design for a bedroom by Gertrud Kleinhempel for the Dresdener Werkstätten of Hellerau c.1902. The simplicity of the forms, emphasizing good materials, sound construction and practical utility, were characteristics of the workshops founded in many German cities in the early years of the century. (*courtesy* R.I.B.A.)

Coffee service by Henry van der Velde for the Royal Saxon Porcelain Manufactory, Meissen, c.1905. (courtesy: Badisches Landesmuseum, Karlsruhe)

A range of clocks from Stukenbrok's 1912 catalogue, which used a standard mechanism but varied casings to suit whatever taste the market desired.

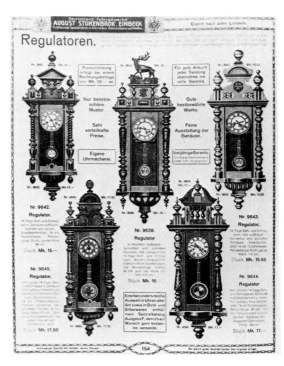

Plate, part of a dinner service, by Richard Riemerschmid for the Royal Saxon Porcelain Manufactory, Meissen, 1905. (courtesy: Badisches Landesmuseum, Karlsruhe)

A half-page from the August Stukenbrok mail-order catalogue of 1912, illustrating the *Arminius* racing-cycle, offered with full guarantee and cost-free return if it was not satisfactory.

The *Deutschland* sewing-machine built on the Singer system, offered in the Stukenbrok 1912 mail-order catalogue. The cost of the machine, table and treadle mechanism was approximately the same as the *Arminius* bicycle.

founder, was established in 1890 as a small bicycle manufactory, when Stukenbrok recognized the market potential of the new form of transport. Under brand names such as 'Deutschland', 'Arminia' and 'Teutonia', which all had a nationalist ring, he went on to expand into the production of sewing machines and automobile accessories, using intense advertising methods, and eventually began to bulk buy other products as a basis for a mail-order business. By 1911, regular customers numbered over 600,000 and a million catalogues were sent out annually. Custom on such a scale would indicate that Stukenbrok's products mirrored the tastes of a substantial proportion of the population.

In over 230 pages in the 1912 catalogue there is no hint of influence from any aspect of the cultural reform movement. Neither is there any consistent pattern in the massive range of goods available, extending from plain, technical products to the most florid, decorative whimsy. Cycles still constituted an important segment of Stukenbrok's own production and they were utilitarian, the frames of welded seamless tube, with any visual effect stemming mainly from a contrast of materials, as with the nickel plated handlebars, front fork and chain wheel. In comparison, the 'Deutschland' sewing machine, intended for domestic use hardly had a surface free from decorative treatment, an approach typical of a majority of products. Cutlery was available with plain handles, for hotel use, but also in a bewildering variety of styles, *Jugendstil*, Empire, Rococo, *Biedermeier* and a series of indeterminate mixtures. Perhaps the most bizarre range was of wall-clocks, in cases displaying every trick of carving and turning to pile up effect and create a range of differentiated housings for standard mechanisms. The immense contrast between the overheated sentimentality of such products and the stark functionality of others, such as cameras, binoculars, tools, automatic pistols and sports equipment is bewildering and

highly inconsistent. It seems obvious that the formal criteria considered suitable for different contexts and activities were compartmentalized, in total contradiction of the unified culture to which the cultural reform movement aspired.

The difficulties encountered by representatives of new artistic tendencies in their work for industrial and commercial concerns were reflected in the concern widely expressed about the relationship. Alexander Koch estimated that the influence of manufacturers, retailers and public was ten times as powerful as that of the artist, who, whilst giving of his best, found 'the value of his goods determined by the market.' [127] When the public was only interested in new fashions, and industry in speculation, how asked Koch, could an artist have cultural interest if his work became a mass-product? It was precisely this problem that dominated both the theory and practice of design in the early years of the century, and which eventually led to deep division in the reform movement, reflecting very different concepts of the relationship of art to contemporary society.

9   Workshops and the adaptation of craft ideas

A sofa designed by Gertrud Kleinhempel for Theophil Müller's workshop in Dresden, c.1901.

Around the turn of the century, a number of talented women designers began to gain recognition in Germany. Two of the foremost, Gertrude Kleinhempel and Margarete Junge, co-operated on this set of white lacquered garden furniture for Karl Schmitt's Dresdener Werkstätten c.1901. (courtesy: RIBA)

Settee by Margarete Junge for the Dresdener Werkstätten c.1900.

In 1890, William Morris published his utopian novel, 'News from Nowhere'. This envisaged a society in which factories had been replaced by 'Banded-workshops', where 'folk collect . . . to do hand-work in which working together is necessary or convenient.' [128] The reverence for craftsmanship and the principle of joy in work were not easily realized, however, and in practical terms required some compromising of ideals. In the English Arts and Crafts Movement, artists such as C.F.A. Voysey and W.R. Lethaby were not executants, but had skilled craftsmen carry out their designs.

Something of the same pattern was evident in Germany. The title of *Vereinigte Werkstätten* was an attempt to translate the term used by Morris, but rather than the practice of crafts being its primary rationale, it was established to make the skills and expertise of craftsmen available to artists, and under control of the latter, which was quite another matter. However, on that basis the example was widely followed in a large number of similar organizations that sprang up in the early twentieth century.

In Dresden, Theodor Müller established his *Werkstätten für deutschen Hausrat* (Workshops for German Furnishings), which although overshadowed by the Hellerau undertaking, nevertheless established a high reputation with designs by Gertrud Kleinhempel, Margarete Junge and Max Nicolai. Similarly in Munich, Karl Bertsch, Adalbert Niemayer and Willy von Beckerath set up the *Münchener Werkstätten für Wohnungs-Einrichtung* (Munich Workshops for Domestic Furnishings). This later merged with the *Dresdener Werkstätten* in 1907 under the new designation of the *Deutsche Werkstätten*, though on account of its size, Hellerau was the dominant partner with Karl Schmidt assuming overall control. Elsewhere in the

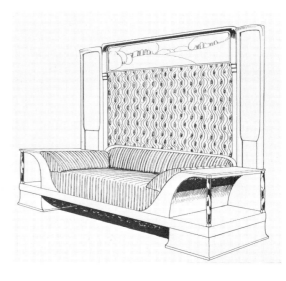

Living-room designed by Max Nicolai for the *Werkstätten für Deutschen Hausrat* founded by Theophil Müller in Dresden. Though less well-known than its Hellerau neighbour, Müller's products were of a consistently high standard. (courtesy: RIBA)

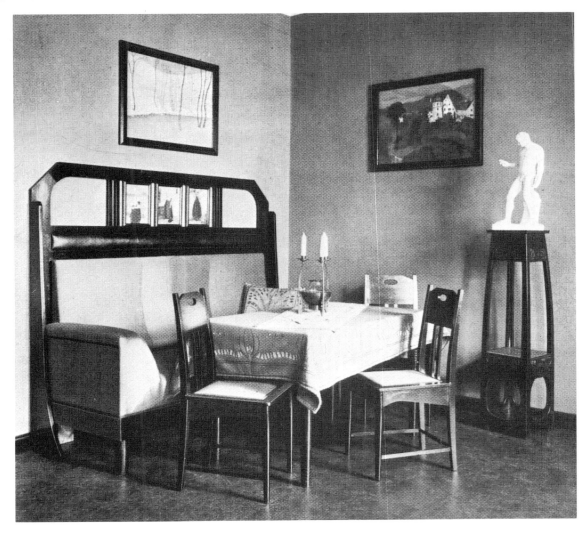

country, however, there were many similar undertakings of varying size and range of specialization, such as the *Paderborner Werkstätten* established by Bernhard Stadler, many of whose furniture designs were by Max Heidrich, a local architect, or Hans Kramer of Marne in Holstein who drew upon regional models in his workshop production.

Common to all these undertakings, irrespective of size, was the belief that hand-made domestic fittings of high quality, expressing an artist's personality, had an important com-plementary role to the bland, mass-manufac-tured products of industry. They could offer something individual and special, often of a local nature, which combined function and aesthetics.

However, although the technical basis of many smaller undertakings remained that of hand-work, there were also developments that moved a significant stage beyond the mediaeval ideal of Morris, adapting to modern conditions and opportunities. In Munich, Wilhelm Debschitz established a *Lehr*

94

Part of a kitchen designed by Willy von Beckerath for the *Münchener Werkstätten für Wohnungs Einrichtungen* c.1904. Von Beckerath's work was characterized by clean lines and fine proportions. (courtesy: RIBA)

In addition to the workshops which became large businesses, others were founded or developed from existing craft undertakings which contributed substantially to broadening the influence of the cultural reform movement. An advertisement for the Applied Art Workshops of Koblinsky & Co of Breslau dating from 1901 shows a bedroom suite in the then fashionable *Jugendstil*. (courtesy: RIBA)

— und Versuchs-Atelier für Angewandte und Freie Kunst (Teaching and Research Studio for Applied and Free Art) in 1903, an independent teaching establishment in which the ideas of Hermann Obrist strongly influenced the programme. The study of nature, its laws rather than its appearance, was the heart of Debschitz's educational philosophy. He attempted to avoid any definitions of right or wrong, taking students through a sequence of work from the most simple to those requiring complete mastery, emphasizing individual tuition and development.

Parallel to his teaching activity, Debschitz was also a partner in the *Ateliers und Werkstätten für Angewandte Kunst,* (Studios and Workshops for Applied Art), which on one level produced a limited range of craft products for private commission, but more significantly, also acted as a consultant design organization, preparing designs and models for firms of all sizes. The philosophy behind this combination of activity, was that practical work was necessary to give artists

KOBLINSKY & C⁰., BRESLAU.

KUNSTGEWERBLICHE WERKSTÄTTEN.

Dining-room armchair in oak with woven fabric seat by Richard Riemerschmid and executed by the Dresdener Werkstätten in 1902. (courtesy: Badisches Landesmuseum, Karlsruhe)

Corner of the Speaker's room in the Saxon State Assembly building in Dresden with furnishings designed by Richard Riemerschmid for the *Dresdener Werkstätten* in 1903. Such commissions by a regional government indicate the rapid growth in prestige and recognition of the *Werkstätten* since its foundation five years earlier.

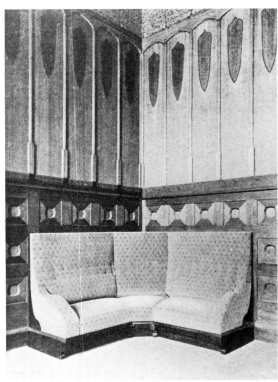

and modellers experience of the total process of production, which would keep them fresh for the design work undertaken for industrial companies. In this way, the values of artists who were practically competent could be given wider scope, influencing taste through the medium of industry. A similar pattern was evident in the *Lehr-und Versuchs Atelier* (Teaching and Research Studio) established at the Stuttgart School of Applied Art under the direction of Bernhard Pankok.

If some workshops sought a closer relationship with industry, the two banner-carriers of the new movement, the *Dresdener* and *Vereinigte Werkstätten,* were so successful that both grew into major commercial undertakings with substantial production facilities, though still giving predominance of the role of artists in the production process.

At Hellerau, rapid growth was accompanied by an increasing use of mechanization in production. Schmidt regarded machines simply as another type of tool, emphasizing an understanding of them and their appropriate use, though their application was regarded as supplemental to, rather than a replacement of handwork.

In the early years of the new century, many artists continued to work with Schmidt, but it was Richard Riemerschmid who was responsible for the most significant developments in Hellerau designs. He had trained as an artist in Munich and had been a leading member of the *Jugendstil* movement there. By 1900, the influence of that style was waning, and from this time forward, the greater portion of his output was for Hellerau. An oak chair of 1902 showed only vestigial traces of *Jugendstil* influence, relying on material quality and straightforward, sound construction for effect, only the chamfered legs and back support relieving the solid outline. By 1906, Riemer-

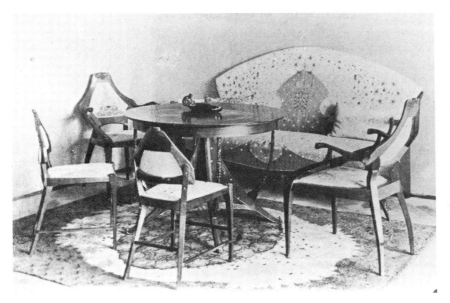

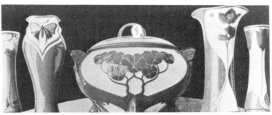

Lounge furniture designed for the *Vereinigte Werkstätten,* Munich, by Bernhard Pankok c.1901.

Tea-service by Jan Eisenlöffel for the *Vereinigte Werkstätten,* c.1908. (courtesy: Badisches Landesmuseum, Karlsruhe)

A range of porcelain wares by Theo Schmuz-Baudiss for the *Vereinigte Werkstätten,* Munich, c.1901.

schmid was producing 'build-on' furniture, such as a sideboard consisting of three separate elements, the cupboard and drawer units to left and right being compatible but optional items. Stylistically, these drew more on traditional forms associated with the Arts and Crafts revival, being plain and finely proportioned, the only decorative effect-derived from the grain of smoked oak and the metal fittings.

Both the chair and sideboard were craft-made in fine materials, but also in 1906, the *Dresdener Werkstätten* produced a range of machine-made furniture from Riemerschmid's designs. Their basic box-like structure was well-adapted to mechanized serial-production, using plain materials, veneers often replacing solid timber, though the attention to detail and general standards of quality were maintained. Some was produced in 'knock-down' form for ease and lower cost of transportation, for assembly at the point of sale. By contemporary standards, their cost was low, a basic three room fitting costing 570 RM, providing a significant demonstration of the possibility of aesthetic and functional quality in mechanized production. Its inspiration was

the social idealism of Karl Schmidt, who realized an emphasis on craft work alone would mean limited production at high cost. In his belief that standards of quality could be maintained, provided designs were appropriate to machines and not used as a cheap surrogate for craft work, he took a significant step beyond the emphasis current in the English Arts and Crafts movement. His social aim was to provide good and simple furniture for a wide section of the population, though in practice this generally meant a middle-class market sympathetic to the aims of cultural reform.

The *Vereinigte Werkstätten* was less inspired by social idealism, but was no less successful. Founded in 1897, it grew rapidly in the early 1900s with a reputation for quality work by talents such as Bernhard Pankok, Th. Th. Heine and, above all, Bruno Paul, who designed hundreds of pieces including furniture, light fittings and domestic implements of all kinds.

Around 1900, Paul's work was still predominantly in a restrained version of *Jugendstil,* but it subsequently evolved to more rectangular forms that reminded some critics of the solid burger quality of the Bieder-

Sideboard by Bruno Paul
for the *Vereinigte
Werkstätten* c.1909. One
of Paul's 'build-on'
designs this consists of
three separate units. Full-
length cupboards were
also available, a
selection of units being
able to fit together in
varying configurations.

A sideboard designed by
Bruno Paul for the
Vereinigte Werkstätten
c.1907, illustrating his use
of laminated timber sheet
to produce a curved
frontal surface.

The external form of the modern ocean liner crystalized in the 1890s. The Hamburg-Amerika liner *Deutschland* won the Blue Riband on its maiden voyage to New York in 1901. The exteriors of such vessels aroused great interest in design circles as an expression of technical aesthetics. Like all Hamburg-America ships of that period, however, the *Deutschland* was fitted out with sumptuous interiors in a range of historical styles.

meier period of the early nineteenth century.

Initially the *Vereinigte Werkstätten* relied upon hand-work for production, beginning with a staff of four which increased within a year to fifty. By 1905, however, Paul was experimenting with a concept of unit-furniture derived from the modular bookcases produced by the American firm, Globe-Wernicke. The material Paul utilized was laminated timber sheets, which when pressed in special moulds, were capable of producing curved surfaces. The result was not an expression of the logic of machine production, but a subordination of it to Paul's aesthetic concepts, the concave and convex surfaces he demanded causing enormous difficulties in setting-up the machinery, which required expensive moulds, and with many problems in manufacture. Function and production technique, however, although important, were never determinants for Paul, rather a point of departure, offering opportunities for expression.

Paul's 'build-on' system basically consisted of side-pieces, doors, drawers and compartments. For chests and cupboards these could be assembled as 'furniture cells', with five different sizes offering varied combinations but maintaining formal unity. The finishes available were varnished or lacquered pine, veneered oak, birch or mahogany in matt or polished finish. By 1910, two different systems were each available for dining rooms, boudoirs and studies and there were three bedroom sets. Yet despite the innovatory techniques employed, the result was expensive, representative furniture, undeniably of high quality, which, like all Paul's work at this time, sought to preserve links with the past without becoming directly imitative. It was this vein of conservatism allied to modern techniques, however, that made his furniture appealing.

The growth of the workshops into substantial businesses and in gaining acceptance can be gauged by the scale of commissions they executed. The success of *Dresdener Werkstätten* in obtaining continuous work for

the Imperial Navy, was subsequently followed by substantial commissions from commercial shipping lines.

The contrast between the external and internal forms of warships referred to earlier were equally valid for passenger ships. Leading artists had been employed for designs since the 1880s and several leading furniture manufacturers were specialists in ships' fittings, for example, A. Bembé of Mainz, whose approach can be judged from the fact that in addition to ships, it furnished villas for Krupp, Thyssen and other large industrialists, as well as castles for King Karl of Rumania and Duke Ferdinand of Bulgaria. Over the years it had been responsible for the first-class fitting of a long list of vessels for the Hamburg Amerika line, including the *Hamburg* and *Augusta Viktoria II*, and North German Lloyd, including the *Kaiser Wilhelm der Grosse* and *Prinz Ludwig*. The latter typified prevailing concepts of rich luxury manifested in a surfeit of historical decoration.

The designs were by J.G. Poppe of Bremen, architect to N.G.L., which included, for example, a dining-room executed by Bembé in Louis XVI style.

When a change of approach set in, it was due to the influence of the General Director of North German Lloyd, Dr Heinrich Wiegand. He developed a sympathy for modern tendencies in the applied arts and wanted Bruno Paul to take over responsibility for the interior fittings of the line's new ships. Paul's appointment to the Berlin School of Applied Art prevented this. However, Wiegand did organize a competition in which leading artists were invited to submit designs for a new liner, the *Kronprinzessin Cäcilie*, which had its maiden voyage in August, 1907. Poppe, then seventy years of age, was still responsible for the majority of public rooms and fittings on this vessel. 'For him the basis of his decorative art remains sacrosanct, the imitation of old stylistic forms, emanating from ornament.' [129] The dining-room in Renaissance, an upper-deck cafe in Louis XVI, and the saloon in Empire-style indicated the range of his taste. What aroused a sense of excitement in commentators, however, was the outcome of the earlier competition initiated by Wiegand in a series of forty luxury cabins, in which a younger generation were able to specify designs to the last detail. They were divided between Bremen practitioners, such as Runge and Scotland, and Wellermann and Fröhlich, and a selected number of modern practitioners such as Riemerschmid, Olbrich and Paul. The work was executed by the *Vereingte* and *Dresdener Werkstätten*, Gebr. Bauer of Berlin, Schneider and Hanau, and Pallenberg of Cologne. In breaking away from historical pomp, these cabins indicated new possibilities that were developed on a larger scale in subsequent vessels.

Commissions for ships-fittings were not only prestigious but highly profitable and there was considerable rivalry and competition for this business between the *Vereinigte* and

Deutsche Werkstätten. Bruno Paul's relationship with Wiegand seems to have been decisive in giving the former an advantage, and in 1908 it established a branch in Bremen specifically to service this work. There followed a share in work for the *Derfflinger* in 1907, and in the following year N.G.L. placed in service the *Prinz Friedrich Wilhelm* and the *George Washington*. For the former, Paul designed the first-class dining-room and saloon, with associated ante-rooms and staircases. His ability to use the structure of the ship as the basis of his decorative concepts aroused particular comment. 'The structural skeleton is not concealed, it is visible, but one feels it not as raw material, for it has become part of a linear network of decorative significance.' [130] For the *George Washington*, a larger number of rooms and cabins was commissioned from the *Vereinigte Werkstätten* and F.A.O. Krüger and Rudolf Schröder joined Paul in preparing

Vienna Cafe for smokers on the NGL liner *Kronprinzessin Cecilie* of 1907. Designed by J.G. Poppe and executed by W. Kümmel of Berlin. (courtesy: RIBA)

designs. Paul recognized the problem as a need to create a sense of spaciousness within confined limits, which required simplified forms and a careful consideration of proportions. An important technique he employed was the avoidance of shadow-effect through the widespread use of smooth surfaces, which gave a feeling of lightness. Furniture was as often as possible built into corners and niches, and rather than ornament, the play of materials, texture, light and colour were effectively employed to give a varied, and often a sumptuous, effect. Krüger's work followed Paul's model but Schröder's contribution was considered less successful in corresponding to the theme of modern ship design: 'Over everything Schroder makes . . . hangs a cloud of Rococco and modish perfume.'[131]

An innovation on the *George Washington*, in which the designers of the first-class areas were not involved, was the provision of third-class accommodation with the purpose of separating 'central European emigrants from those of the east and south. As passengers, German workers, foremen, also young craftsmen and salesmen are anticipated. They will find here hygienically unobjectionable, thoroughly solid and respectable accommodation.'[132]

Although Paul's designs were regarded as particularly successful for their rejection of historicism, the problem of finding an analogue in interior design for the striking technical imagery of ship exteriors was not entirely resolved. The interiors were intended to attract the custom of wealthy passengers,

First-class lounge designed by Bruno Paul and executed by the *Vereinigte Werkstätten* for the NGL liner *George Washington* of 1908.

and luxury, or the lack of it, was an index of how much had been paid to travel in a particular class.

Paul was himself entirely clear about this. In an article published in 1914, he contrasted the clarity and confidence evident in ship construction with the excessive expenditure of money, materials and effort on interiors that were unsatisfying. The increased proportions of modern vessels, he said, brought new possibilities, 'giving travellers the illusion of a stay in a building on firm land.' [133] The characteristic configuration of ships, with their curving outer lines, imposed particular spatial constraints, but Paul considered there were no limits to the materials available for interior designs. Since there were not special artistic or technical difficulties, it was only necessary to follow the same successful logic of technical construction to reach 'the most functional, most simple, most obvious and most

natural form. So one has to apply correct principles for ships' fittings, in order to achieve practicality, useability and the utmost comfort, and a certain elegance corresponding to our mode of life, our habits and our own appearance . . . The spaces should not only appear comfortable and elegant, but rich too, and should have something special to say to those accustomed to a stay in splendid surroundings.' [134] This could be achieved by using the best of modern decorative art, work that was beautiful and of the highest technical quality. By such means a voyage in the first-class could become 'an artistic delight' in the near future. 'The spaces of the second class will be reserved, satisfying all aesthetic requirements through tasteful practicality, and also in the steerage artistic efforts can be carried through, the cold sobriety of pure construction giving a practical, obvious and simple beauty through colour and form.' [135]

Luxury cabin designed by Bruno Paul and executed by the *Vereinigte Werkstätten* for the NGL liner *Prinz Friedrich Wilhelm* of 1908.

Paul's view was pragmatic and accurate. The first-class passengers demanded value for money and their needs had to be satisfied, though it was the other classes of accommodation which more closely approximated to the ideals of the reformers. However, it needs to be stressed that ships were the only means of transport across the large expanses of ocean separating the continents, providing year-round services under all conditions. Storms and rough seas with their attendant dangers and discomforts were a normal hazard, particularly on the prestigious North Atlantic route. An image of comfortable familiarity could mitigate the fears of potential passengers and reassure sufferers en route.

It was perhaps for such reasons that in 1912, North German Lloyd began to explore other possibilities and for the first time employed Paul Ludwig Troost to design interiors for the *Columbus* which entered service in 1914. Trained as an architect, Troost favoured the simplified neo-classicism which in this period was widely regarded as appropriate for the time. Its simplicity, geometrical clarity and historical links with earlier periods of German culture were amongst the qualities attributed to it. Troost was therefore able to prepare designs for the *Columbus* in a style that satisfied both the desire for contemporaneity and for luxury, and which in its geometrical proportions and emphasis could be considered appropriate to the technical forms enclosing it. The choice of Troost indicated that the ideas of the new movement could not be adequately reconciled with the demand for pomp and luxury in first-class accommodation.

The *Deutsche Werkstätten* found some consolation eventually with a commission from Hamburg-Amerika. Their huge liner *Imperator*, launched in 1913, had been heavily criticized

103

Changing-room and first-class swimming pool on the Hamburg-Amerika liner *Imperator* of 1913. Widespread criticism of its ponderous and archaic interiors led the company's Director, Albert Ballin, to reconsider his faith in lavish historical decor.

for its interiors, which were an unimaginative mixture of decorative styles, and the General Director of the line, Albert Ballin asked Hermann Muthesius for advice. As a result Riemerschmid, Karl Bertsch and Adalbert Niemayer prepared designs for the steamship, *Burckhard,* completed in 1917. Like Paul's work for N.G.L., this rejected historicism but not luxury and display. In this, perhaps more than in any other sphere of activity, the design of ship interiors before the First World War indicated the constraints on innovation by the reformers. Change was indeed possible, but only within very strict limits that did not challenge the social predelictions of the customer. However, the propaganda value of having the work of eminent representatives of the new movement permanently exhibited on major trade routes was apparently a compensation for such constraints.

Another feature of the commercial expansion of both the major workshops was not only the extent of mechanization involved, but the growing range of products they marketed, moving from an initial emphasis on furniture to encompass a total range of domestic fittings, including lighting, textiles and ceramics. In some instances, designs were prepared by artists associated with the workshop and executed by an outside company, as with Max Läuger's ceramic wares for the *Deutsche Werkstätten,* which were produced by Villeroy

& Boch. Sometimes, however, the success of a particular line led to the establishment of new manufacturing facilities, as with the *Deutsche Werkstätten*'s opening of a new workshop solely for the production of toys in 1908. A further index of growth was the opening of the major workshops and showrooms in major cities across the country, thus giving control over quality from concept, through production, to sale.

That exclusivity was also the starting point for another intitiative which extended the influence of the workshop idea, that also originated in Dresden. Arthur Schubert, who owned a furniture showroom in that city, and wished to offer a higher standard of products, had unsuccessfully attempted to persuade Schmidt to allow him to sell the *Deutsche Werkstätten* range, and consequently sought to form an association of furniture-sellers, who would commission their own designs. Such an association of sellers was a completely new idea. At an exhibition in Berlin in May, 1912, 'Women at Home and at Work', he saw furniture design by Lotte Klopsch, who was engaged as the first designer for the new organization. Schubert then entered into a partnership with Edwin Bahr to establish full production facilities at Wendlingen in Würtemburg. By the autumn of 1912, firms in Frankfurt, Königsberg, Düsseldorf, Kiel and Magdeburg had joined the association which was formally established in November of that year, and later took the title of *Deutsche WK-Möbel,* the initials standing for *Wohnungs-Kunst* ('art furnishings'). The first range of furniture produced was highly successful and the number of member-stores expanded in 1913 to eighteen. By 1914, four ranges of furniture were planned and demand so exceeded the capacity of the Wendlingen plant, that a second manufacturer was commissioned with part of the work. Although the association broke down during the First World War due to difficulties in obtaining adequate supplies, Schubert's idea had

proved so successful that it recommenced after the war, but on a vastly expanded scale.

It was not only the artefacts produced by the workshops, but also their philosophy which influenced Schubert and his colleagues. This was evident in the foundation document of the association from February 1913, in which their purpose was expressed as developing an 'understanding of the significance of good taste and a thorough cultural education' and 'the creation of a particular style of national character for furniture and objects of interior decoration'. [136] The cultural tone and the attempt to create a unified style were all derived from the example of the *Deutsche Werkstätten*.

In just over a decade after their foundation, the major workshops had become transformed from small associations of artists intent on asserting their role and their standards in production, to large, highly capitalized businesses with a chain of their own outlets. The influence of artists was not only maintained, but expanded, as their design skills were applied to all aspects of the business, to the workplace, sale-rooms and advertising material, as well as artefacts. This emphasis, and their considerable success, presented a permanent challenge to other sectors of industry and commerce, demonstrating that design-led firms could be highly profitable. If success and expansion meant coming to terms with commercial and market constraints, it did not mean the original ideals which inspired the workshops were entirely sacrificed, but oriented and adapted to modern circumstances instead of an image of the past.

10 The Third German Applied Arts Exhibition, Dresden

The ideal of artistic control epitomized by the workshops was also a central concern for a crucial event in coalescing the energies of the varied efforts to reform the applied arts and design: the *III deutsche Kunstgewerbeausstellung* of 1906, on this occasion held in Dresden. It was seminal in several respects, not least because during the exhibition the first suggestions were made for a permanent body to further the reform movement.

The main impetus for this idea appears to have stemmed from Friedrich Naumann, who emerged in the 1890s as one of Germany's leading liberal politicians. A former Protestant pastor who became active in politics through the Christian Social movement, he formed a new party in 1896, the National Social Union, which was intended to bridge the gulf between the working classes and the bourgeoisie, between labour and capital, and create a new national unity. He believed that patriotism could heal social division, and to this end supported a forward foreign policy, the acquisition of colonies, and military and naval expansion, as a means of augmenting Germany's role in the world and giving a focus to national feeling. In his vision of a strong, united Germany, respected and honoured in the world, he hoped for a strengthening of parliamentary government with the participation of all sections of society, which led him to support womens' suffrage, a rare and brave stance in contemporary German politics. Naumann failed to attract any appreciable support, however, the working-classes being suspicious of an ideal of unity which blended imperialism with a proletarian concept stripped of Marxism, and his party was dissolved in 1903. He subsequently became active in the liberal Progressive Party. Despite his lack of political success, however, Naumann attracted a large follow-ing throughout Germany amongst the middle-class youth, which included the sociologist Max Weber, the historian Friedrich Meinecke, and Theodor Heuss, active in liberal political and literary circles. An important instrument for his ideas was a journal he founded in 1894, *Die Hilfe,* in which in addition to urging better understanding between the classes, he developed the theme of the implications for Germany of developments in literature and the visual arts. It was in this journal that in 1904 he published an important article, 'Art in the Age of the Machine', which called for industrial methods of production to be used to create new forms expressing the spirit of the time.

His vision of social and national renewal laid great stress on the role of aesthetics, and in particular, the need to positively harness the potential of mechanization. In his writings he logically analysed the essential differences between craft and industrial production, pointing out in an address during the Dresden exhibition that whereas three activities of artist, producer and salesman were united in the person of the craftsman, the artist was now separated from the businessman, who in turn separated the productive and retail parts of his activity. Naumann believed that to manufacture hand products by mechanical means would only debase both work and product, emphasizing: 'Multiple reproduction is the basic concept of industrial art.'[137] Germany, he argued, had produced a number of commercial artists of high standing precisely at the point where 'the systematic reproduction of artistic discovery has become a specific professional activity.' Machine-produced articles could be beautiful, but to generally achieve this 'the machine must be spiritualized' and used by entrepreneurs 'as an educator of taste.'[138] Exploiting the possibilities of mech-

Despite the efforts of reformers, historically based forms remained popular, often in eclectic combinations, such as this lavish bath and dressing-room for Schloss Hünegg near Thun in Switzerland by the prestigious firm of A. Bembé of Mainz in 1904. (*courtesy* R.I.B.A.)

Dining-room for the Westend house, Berlin, by Bruno Paul, 1909, executed by the Berlin branch of the Vereinigte Werkstätten. The light airy atmosphere and subtle harmonies of colour and form in this room, with variations of grid and lattice patterns, show Paul's assurance after well over a decade of applied art designing.

Wintergarden with fountain designed by Max Kühne with ceramic tiles and containers by Villeroy & Boch for the Third German Applied Arts Exhibition in Dresden, 1906

reform movement, as a result of which a young supporter of Naumann's, Wolf Dohrn, was given the task of preparing the ground for a new organization. The subsequent crystallization of these activities in the foundation of the *Deutscher Werkbund* has frequently overshadowed accounts of the Dresden exhibition, but the latter was also significant in other respects which deserve consideration. Above all, it marked a decisive change in the organisation of such exhibitions, since for the first time an element of control was exercised over what was exhibited and by whom.

The organizational committee included Wilhelm Lossow, an established Dresden architect as chairman, Karl Gross and Otto Seyffert, a painter as vice-chairman and secretary, and amongst bankers, engineers and museum directors the membership included Cornelius Gurlitt, Erich Kleinhempel, Max Kühne, Wilhelm Kreis and Fritz Schumacher, all active in the architectural and applied art life of Dresden. Practitioners dominated the committee numerically and from the earliest stages imposed a strongly programmatic character on the exhibition. In a brief introduction outlining the plans issued prior to the exhibition, Lossow wrote: 'Because we will be endeavouring to keep from the exhibition everything that could disturb the taste-forming character of it, we therefore request you also to be effective in this sense in your district for the promotion of German applied art.'[139] In effect, the exhibition was to be limited to modern tendencies and artists were to be the arbiters of what was acceptable. In previous events organizations and companies had been able to book space and exhibit what they wanted. At Dresden, only artists exhibited, and firm's products were only shown through the choice and agency of artists. For example, tiles and ceramic products of the firm of Villeroy & Boch were used by Max Kühne in the Wintergarden he designed. They were highly praised, but the

anization was not an end in itself, however, for with an increasing population, he argued, Germany needed simultaneously to give workers a sense of national pride and fulfilment to counteract the influence of socialism, and open up world markets for its products. Quality work and good form were therefore advocated as indispensable elements of achieving social unity domestically and international commercial competitiveness. In rejecting any concept of 'art for art's sake' in favour of 'industrial art' as part of the mainstream of contemporary social and economic policy, Naumann brought a powerful sense of purpose to many practitioners — Karl Schmidt, for example, was a disciple of his and the policies operated at Hellerau can be viewed as a practical manifestation of Naumann's ideas. Once identified with such a programme, however, there was henceforward a danger of the applied arts becoming the overt subject of political controversy and manipulation.

At Dresden, Naumann and Karl Schmidt held discussion with other leaders of the

Mantelpiece and
furniture in the saloon of
the Saxon House
designed by Wilhelm
Kreis for the 1906
Dresden Exhibition.

firm itself did not exhibit in its own right. In practice, the influence of such companies was considered but even the *Dresdener Werkstätten* participated as an association of artists.

In the organizational programme, for which Schumacher was largely responsible, advances in both craft and industrial production were acknowledged, but the frequent confusion of the two was deemed to require clarification. The improvement of public taste for a greater understanding was also stressed. To provide a survey of contemporary trends, however, required the organization to recognize different points of view, which were reflected in the conceptual structure. The sections proposed were:

I The Visual Arts

This was not only to present an overview of painting and sculpture, but by exhibiting works in settings, to show their role in everyday life. Many would therefore be shown in the context of interior designs. The intention was to exhibit interiors as ensembles, showing how all the arts could be combined into an harmonious environment.

II Arts and Crafts

The intention was not to exhibit single items as objets d'art, but to show the riches of hand work. It was therefore to be subdivided into:

a. Folk art of different regions that 'remains fresh in the changes of historical styles'.

b. How objects develop from the inner laws of materials uninterrupted by stylistic change.

c. How this heritage can be further developed in schools dedicated to the crafts.

d. Objects grouped to show the character of city and region.

III Art Industry

This section was to emphasize the machine

as a tool for the execution of artistic designs. 'One of the most important contemporary cultural tasks exists in the creation of such articles of use linked to a healthy path, which in their mass-production control the needs and thereby the taste of our age. For this section the intention is to show selected products of industry, that through mechanical working do not obliterate the beauty of naked materials, or alter to deceive, but as far as possible reveal their value, and also to show the errors induced by the hopeless competition with the decorative forms created by hand.'

The products of leading firms were also to be shown to demonstrate the 'world market interests of industry' and organized according to material categories. Complete rooms would show how mechanical production could serve 'tasteful middle-class needs.'[140]

This structure in fact neatly summarized the different aspects of the reform movement, judiciously giving each its place, but in each

Living-room by Fritz Schumacher in the Saxon House, Dresden Exhibition 1906.

emphasizing the primacy of artistic creativity over other factors. Writing from Dresden just before the exhibition opened, a local writer commented: 'We have an individual art, an art with delicate roots but with firm branches. It draws its powers not from the depths of national feeling, but rests on the work of a series of personalities, in whom the best traits of the national character are embodied.'[141] The artistic image of the event was also promoted by the exhibition poster by Otto Gussmann, in which a symbolic female figure had a small tree of applied art growing from her hand.

The emphasis was therefore on what was considered artically valid, rather than simply commercially viable, and when the exhibition opened, the range of work shown was widely considered to be exemplary and modern.

The Saxon House, for example, one of the main features, designed by Wilhelm Kreis, was highly praised by the critic Albert Hoffman. It was a large building with many rooms, in three of which Kreis designed the interiors, other artists being responsible for the remainder. Kreis himself said of the exhibition: 'Practicality (Sachlichkeit) has been victorious over appearance, without intrusively wanting to state the naked truth.' He rejected both 'parading bravura little pieces of technology or unlimited constructional fantasy.'[142] Clearly, Sachlichkeit for Kreis did not mean a reduction to basic elements the term later signified. His rooms, such as the Salon, were luxurious, but the catalogue stressed that although not typical in this, they sought to be typical in their approach to a solution, this common factor deriving from three elements of a problem: the purpose a room serves, the materials to be used, and the nature of the people creating it. Thus to function and materials was added the artistic personality of its creator. Albert Hoffman wrote of Kreis' work: 'The common element ... lies in an apparently unwilled, unsought, modest individualism, which at the same time reveals a German character in the best sense of the word. The formal language is indepen-

Part of a kitchen designed in 1905 by Richard Riemerschmid for the 'machine-furniture' range of the *Dresdener Werkstätten*. It was made of pine, lacquered grey, with black iron fittings. (courtesy: RIBA)

dent, new and seeks not to powerfully claim the spectator for itself, but limits itself to a discrete, purely practical effect.'[143]

Kreis' designs were executed by craftsmen. In stark contrast were the suites of 'machine-manufactured' furniture produced by the *Dresdener Werkstätten* in 1905 to designs by Riemerschmid, which although extensively using mechanical processes for cutting and profiling, also required considerable hand work in assembly and finishing. Nevertheless, the stress on mechanization was justified, the intention being to demonstrate the potential of serial production to high standards, in quantities and at prices accessible to a wide market. In the *Dresdener Werkstätten* pavilion, not only were complete rooms exhibited (there were seventeen by Riemerschmid), but there was also a complete workshop with wood-working machines used to process the rough planks into component parts that were

then assembled and painted. A finished piece such as a strong, well-built cupboard could be dismantled in five minutes and laid in a manageable pack for transportation if necessary.

Three sets of 'machine-furniture' were produced. The cheapest included furniture for kitchen, living-room and bedroom at a total of 570 Reichmarks. It was made of spruce, stained in various colours. The living-room set, for example, was available stained red or blue, the bedroom set green, the kitchen red. Brass fittings were used for the living-room, where visitors could be expected, but iron sufficed for the privacy of bedroom and kitchen. The structural elements were pegged, and the rounded heads of the pegs were left proud to relieve the plain structure. The frames in cupboards and wardrobes were of solid timber, but the in-fill panels were sheets of laminate, giving a clean flush surface.

A dining-room in the *Dresdener Werkstätten's* machine-furniture range designed by Richard Riemerschmid in 1905. It was in smoked oak with scoured iron fittings. The sideboard in the background consisted of three interchangeable units and is an example of Riemerschmid's development of the 'build-on' concept in his designs. (courtesy: RIBA)

Small stencilled motifs were applied to large surfaces. The second set consisted of a living-dining room in mahogany, bedroom in larch, and the kitchen from the first set with additional items at a cost of 1200 RM. The third set comprised a dining-room and study in oak, living room in mahogany, and bedroom and kitchen as in the second set, all for 2600 RM. Not only were the materials and fittings better in the second and third sets, the quality of workmanship was superior, with structural elements jointed and the polished surfaces more finely treated.

If the intention in this programme to give artistic expression to machine production was one important strand, the emphasis on its social function was also crucial, as was widely emphasized. Paul Schumann was of the opinion: 'This furniture may not be the final solution to the high social task of creating respectable furnishings for the common man, but certainly here a great step forward has been taken, and indeed on the right path: the furniture is on one hand thoroughly solid in construction, and appears on the other hand thoroughly respectable and agreeable.' It was, in summary, 'an artistic and ethical deed.' [144]

Friedrich Naumann, however, had no doubts about this achievement of his protegee, Schmidt, and assessed its social significance in positive and sweeping terms: 'For do we not already see in inferior mass furniture, how different forms can be made with relatively simple machine-components? This inferior art must be refined, the machine must be spiritualized, the combination of elements must be thought through. With this natural entrepreneurial ideal the modern commercial cabinet-maker comes to meet the

Oven doors and cladding designed by Karl Gross and exhibited in the industrial art section of the 1906 Dresden exhibition.

Ships' lanterns designed by F.A. Schutze of Berlin and shown at the 1906 Dresden Exhibition. The catalogue commented they were also exemplary models for domestic lighting purposes.

Machine produced workers' furniture in alder wood designed by Willy Meyer of Dresden and produced by Max Böhme & Co of Dippoldiswalde in Saxony.

innovative artist and the purchasing public... He weans his purchasers away from florid ornament, because he can work better without it. So through the entrepreneur the machine becomes an educator of taste.'[145]

Hermann Muthesius was of like opinion. In the *Dresdener Werkstätten* catalogue of 1906, introducing the programme, he considered such work, with its qualities of simplicity, truth and unpretentiousness, would 'come to be held more important that the so-called artistic.'[146] The latter was specifically identified with the *Jugendstil* heritage of individuality.

Simplicity was equated with classlessness, a striving for individuality was rejected in favour of service to the community. Curiously, however, other exhibits epitomizing the trend of mechanization, and with, in many cases, proven social value were ignored, as they have also subsequently been.

In the smaller of the two industrial halls, Karl Gross organized an exhibition under the slogan: 'The beauty of solid materials, the beauty of genuine work, the beauty of pure functional form.' It included automobiles, motor-cycles, rowing-boats, models of warships; stoves, vending-machines, bathroom and toilet fittings, and ovens in 'exemplary

forms' in which 'the beauty of pure functional form should be proven and also really is proven.'[147]

In the larger hall showing art industry products, among many other sets of furnishings, was one designed by Willy Meyer of Dresden and produced by a Saxon manufacturer, Max Böhme and Co. This too was manufactured by machine processes and was considered not to be as interesting as Riemerschmid's range. Meyer's designs, however, were intended for working-class families and cost 471 RM for bedroom, living-room and kitchen. The cheapest Hellerau range was quoted at 570 RM, though there was a catch in that price. If the wardrobe had two-doors, which gave more adequate access to garments, the total price rose to 640 RM. In modern parlance, the single-door wardrobe could be seen as a 'loss-leader', giving an impression of a lower price than

Two automatic vending machines (left and right) and oven-doors (centre) exhibited in the industrial art section of the 1906 Dresden Exhibition.

originality.' He applauded the respect for tradition evident, believing 'the art of the past must again become a regulator, as it has always been, for a possibly exuberant new creation of the present.' The industrial section, he felt, showed the way towards bringing art into everyday life, though industry generally was castigated for having produced astonishingly little suitable for this exhibition. It either rejected the new art or misunderstood it, asserted Zimmermann, and had neither helped nor promoted it. In general, however, he thought that at Dresden a strong programme had been consistently executed and resulted in an extraordinary achievement.[149]

The sections for the traditional, regional crafts have also been frequently overlooked in subsequent accounts, but once again, found advocates at the time.

At a conference of organizations for folk-art and folk-lore also held in Dresden in October, 1906, the main address by Professor Fuchs of Freiburg was on 'The Economic Significance of Folk Art', which referred to the exhibition just closed. *Heimatkunst,* or native art, he argued, ensured that culture had an indigenous foundation. Its modern role was in terms of 'education of manual skill, the schooling of the eye and perceptual capacity in skilled work' and was particularly important in giving those who left the country to work in cities a firm grounding. What was interesting about Fuchs's address was the attempt to justify folk art not in terms of a separate, discrete entity, but in a role relevant to modern development. Both in the attempt to integrate folk art into the wider purposes of the economy and state, and in his xenophobia, he put forward arguments similar to those adopted in advocating Riemerschmid's 'machine' furniture.[150]

The Dresden exhibition was undoubtedly a considerable success, but not all the reaction was favourable. Ernst Zimmermann commented somewhat obliquely: 'That there are also some circles in Germany who are so

was generally the case. The price margin was highly significant in the context of average earnings, which for 90% of Berlin workers in 1907, lay between 900 and 3000 Marks per year.[148] The most expensive set of Riemerschmid's machine furniture would therefore have cost at least more than a year's income for most of the population.

The industrial exhibits and Meyer's designs in particular, however, lacked the cachet of those vital ingredients, a known name with an artistic reputation, or at the very least, a pretension to artistic status.

Riemerschmid's furniture and the speeches of Naumann and Muthesius have frequently been used as justification for interpretations of the Dresden exhibition's significance in terms of the reconciliation of art and technology. Much contemporary comment, even that sympathetic to the new movement, was more in tune with Hoffmann, however, perceiving the emergence, through the creative talent of individual artists, of the long sought national style.

Ernst Zimmermann thought at best there was an assured level of achievement reflecting a generally high level of culture, 'free of grey theory as well as a seeking for unhappy with the exhibition, that they have themselves taken steps to bring discredit on it as the work of a·bungling clique and artistic presumption, is of no significance. They are becoming fainter and fainter, without finding the strong echo for which they had hoped, and can thus pass for the last cry of distress from a party over which the new age rolls with all its might.'[151] Indeed, behind the plaudits a crisis was simmering that boiled over in the following year. Many firms excluded by the restrictions on participation saw their existence threatened and protested vehemently through the *Fachverband für die wirtschaftlichen Interressen des Kunstgewerbes* (Trade association for the economic interests of applied art). This body represented the traditional element of applied art production, the craft businesses based predominantly on hand-processes. They were already under severe pressure from the machine-made products of industry, and the attempt, as they saw it, by artists to insert themselves into a controlling position over what was produced and how it was presented aroused bitter resentment. This was fuelled by their exclusion from exhibiting at Dresden due to the restriction that only artists could do so.

The organization of the Dresden exhibition might therefore have been provocative, but it does not alone account for the vehemence of the *Fachverband's* reaction. It can be seen as but one stage in a running battle that had been taking place between artists who believed in the new movement and established bodies since the 1890s. The Secession societies that had sprung up in the many cities in the *Jugendstil* period — again following the model established in Vienna — had presented a boisterous challenge to established academies and art institutions. The educational changes which began in the early years of the new century also seemed to favour artists, and had been introduced without reference to bodies such as the *Fachverband* and their needs, as they saw them.

Hermann Muthesius, in particular, was widely resented for using his official post and influence in government to promote the new tendencies. The *Fachverband*, under Hermann Hirschwald's leadership, had been regarded as the representative body speaking for the art industries, and it was now being pushed aside. The accumulated resentment against artists' attempts to assert their primacy was simply gunpowder awaiting a spark. This was provided by an inaugural lecture made by Hermann Muthesius in January 1907 at the Berlin *Handelshochschule* (Berlin Commercial University) where he had been appointed Professor of Applied Art. Under the title of *Die Bedeutung des Kunstgewerbes* (The Significance of Applied Art) he reviewed the Dresden exhibition and its success as the starting point for a sweeping programme of reform in the Applied Arts.[152]

Muthesius began by pointing to the common interests of applied art and commerce, expressing the hope that the significance of the former would be included in the curricula of the institution. The meaning of applied art, he asserted, was simultaneously artistic, cultural and economic. The artistic meaning was clear from the Dresden exhibition which had rejected historicism and revealed a new, original artistic language, appropriate to the spiritual, material and social conditions of the age. An inner veracity was a characteristic of this transformation: 'No imitation of any kind, each object appears as what it is, each material reveals its character in its appearance.'

The social significance was not yet clear, said Muthesius, and in this context applied art had an educational task of enormous significance, 'to lead the present social classes back to genuineness, veracity and domestic simplicity . . . It wants to change not only the German home and German house, but to directly influence the character of the generation . . .'

The economic significance of applied art,

however, lay in the future and would be difficult to realize if continually opposed on purely pecuniary grounds. Muthesius cited the *Dresdener Werkstätten* as a profitable and economic concern, but argued it was motivated from the heart, not by money. If the motivation was pure, so would the style that expressed it be pure. The full realization of this required a change of attitude, however, for industralists had failed to consider moral or ethical aims in their businesses. Production must reject superficiality, taking into account the good instincts of the public, and by raising the quality of products, also improve the reputation of German goods in world markets. He referred to the English example in glowing terms and emphasized: 'Commercial success marches in step with the ruling inner values... With great cultural qualities it is easy for a country to assume leadership in the applied arts, to develop its best in freedom and to impose it on the world at the same time.' Artistic development was therefore emphasized in terms of its moral and cultural significance and, as with Naumann, specifically linked to questions of national prestige in world trade.

His lecture aroused a furious response from the *Fachverband*. In a review of contemporary art in Würtemburg, Max Dietz commented that opposition from manufacturers who were *Fachverband* members, mostly in the furniture trade, had seriously affected artists in Stuttgart in a manner he felt both 'painful and shameful'. Indeed at a conference of the *Fachverband* in Berlin in early 1907, a Stuttgart industrialist denounced the attempts of a 'domineering group of artists' to impose their values and demanded that they 'be got rid of.'[153].

The main focus of resentment, however, remained Muthesius, who was branded 'an enemy of German art'. Strenuous efforts were made to have his ministry prevent him making public statements, and his dismissal as professor was demanded of the *Handelshoch-*

schule. The latter request was firmly rejected in a reply which began by stressing that Muthesius had not misused academic freedom. 'Such a critique of previous achievement,' it continued, 'and the indication of means for further development in new paths is not only unharmful for trade and industry, but in high measure beneficial, indeed necessary. Further, no kind of proof that this has taken place in an offensive form has been produced in the case before us.' The reply finally expressed deep regret at the tone of the accusation against this 'most highly esteemed man of German applied art.'[154] The Prussian Ministry of Trade also declined to act on the accusation.

Muthesius' case had been supported by Karl Schmidt, whose *Dresdener Werkstätten* was a member of the *Fachverband*, and he organized a counter-petition defending the stance Muthesius had taken. This brought recriminations from the *Fachverband*, and a bitter exchange of letters followed between its executive and the dissenting firms. In early June, 1907, in that month's issue of the journal *Hohe Warte* there was a report on the 'modern firms', at the instigation of the *Dresdener Werkstätten*, making a statement that indicated a decisive breach in the relationship: 'They will by all means, now and in the future, dispute the right of the *Fachverband* to be considered the authorized representative of the applied arts.'[155] Assuming that statement was made in May in order to appear in print by early June, it seems obvious that Schmidt had already decided to withdraw from the *Fachverband*.

Matters came to a head at the *Fachverband* annual conference in Düsseldorf on June 14th. In a debate on 'The Muthesius Case', as the affair was now grandly called, a handful of speakers defended Muthesius' character and convictions. They were Peter Bruckmann, head of a family cutlery and metalware firm in Heilbronn, who had been invited to the conference, though not a member, to represent the modern standpoint; Joseph August Lux, a writer on applied art but there representing Karl Bertsch's Werkstätten and the Royal Porcelain Manufactory, Nymphenburg; and Dr Wolf Dohrn representing the *Dresdener Werkstätten*. All three spoke in favour of Muthesius's ideas, creating considerable unrest by doing so, and Dohrn concluded: 'But you will see, the modern endeavours will find another representative organization that will serve it better and more usefully and represent applied art and more worthily, than is possible on your side.' He thereupon announced the resignation of the *Dresdener Werkstätten* from the *Fachverband*. Lux too supported the idea of an association to protect artistic interests and stated the *Fachverband* was not capable of protecting the interests of applied art. 'The public will decide,' he said, 'where the retrogressive tendencies lie. It will not be decided in this room, what you and what we are worth, it will be shown in practice, and there we will meet as frequently as possible.' He finally announced the withdrawal of the two firms he represented. The three then walked out.

In an article written almost a quarter of a century later on which most accounts of the event are based and the above quotations are taken, Bruckmann contrived an impression of a spontaneous reaction, stating he had never met his two co-protesters and was seated with them 'quite by accident'.[156] However, he was a committed political supporter of Naumann, who in that same year was elected Reichstag member for Bruckmann's home city of Heilbronn. In his business life, he also attempted to realize Naumann's ideas, emphasizing the need to create modern forms and employing artists such as Rudolf Rochga of the *Lehr- und Versuchs- Atelier,* Stuttgart, to create objects appropriate to machine work. Dohrn was Naumann's protegee representing Schmidt, and his concluding remarks quoted above could be interpreted as prophetic in the context of Bruckmann's article, which omitted to mention that Dohrn had been working for precisely that end on behalf of his mentors for almost a year. Lux was representing Bertsch, who had already decided on the merger with Schmidt to form the *Deutsche Werkstätten,* which was formally announced on July 1st. Lux later worked for Schmidt at Hellerau on the establishment of the garden city there.

Bruckmann's account must therefore be regarded with scepticism as a *post-facto* justification which presented his case in a highly favourable light. The reality of the events between the Dresden exhibition and the Düsseldorf conference would seem to indicate a battle for supremacy and influence. Indeed, Max Osborn wrote an article on the subject under the title, 'The German Applied Art War.' The vehemence of the attacks on Muthesius simply strengthened the resolve of the modernists to vigorously pursue a course already decided on, and they were helped in this by the entrenched position of the *Fachverband*. It is difficult to repress a suspicion that behind the scenes Naumann and Schmidt manipulated a contrived demonstration at Düsseldorf to achieve a break with the *Fachverband,* and so justify the establishment of the new organization determined at Dresden the previous year. Whatever the case, invitations to the founding conference of a new body were despatched with great speed after the *Fachverband* conference.

11 The German *Werkbund*

The invitation to a founding conference of a new organization was signed by twelve artists and twelve representatives of firms. The call was for an association to protect artistic interests, and the composition of the signatories indicated clearly that the workshops established by artists which had grown to such prominence in the previous decade played a decisive role in the crystallization of this idea.[157] About a hundred of those invited gathered in Munich on 6th-7th October, 1907. Originally, the intention was that both Hermann Muthesius and Fritz Schumacher should present an opening address. However, Muthesius decided not to attend owing to the cautious attitude of his ministry following the attacks of the *Fachverband*. The task therefore fell solely to Schumacher.

In his address he posed the question: why was a new organization necessary? He argued that new forces had emerged requiring organization and representation, to avoid the danger of alienation between the spirit of discovery and of execution, between artist and producer. To reconcile these in close, trustful co-operation would benefit both artist and worker. 'We must again recover joy in work, which is synonymous with a raising of quality. And so art is not only an aesthetic, but at the same time, a moral power, both however, leading in the final analysis to the most important of powers: economic power.'[158] The best of innovators, executants and traders should therefore unite to re-establish a harmonious culture. This was essentially a restatement of Friedrich Naumann's views.

The gathering thereafter decided to form a new organization entitled the *Deutsche Werkbund* (German Union of Work) dedicated to the 'improvement of professional work in the co-operation of art, industry and crafts, through education, propaganda and united attitudes to pertinent questions.'

Theodor Fischer was elected Chairman and Peter Bruckmann Vice-Chairman to head a committee of fifteen members.

The purposes of the *Werkbund* were set out in a lengthy memorandum published by the committee following the foundation meeting. It was to be a professional organization, with membership by invitation only, of all those dedicated to commercial work as an element of general cultural endeavours 'under the exclusive recognition of the concept of quality.' This latter theme was a continuous thread throughout the memorandum, and indeed, the whole history of the *Werkbund*. Against the commercial misuse of historical motifs in machine production, was set the idea of quality as the true measure of German culture, expressing 'the striving for harmony, for social discipline, for united leadership of work and life.' This was to be promoted by representing the concept of quality to government and the public, and through the co-operation of art, industry, the crafts and commerce. In particular, the membership was called upon to realize the concept of quality in all aspects of their work. The role of the state was stressed as patron and moulder of public opinion, and above all, education was seen as a vital factor in the realization of the *Werkbund*'s aims, 'for in youth lies constantly the programme of the future.'[159] Exhibitions were also envisaged as a means of creating a demand for quality in a broad circle of consumers. Success in achieving these aims would not only enhance the quality of life and work in Germany, but would bring German products and culture before the eyes of the world. Once again, the unity of national cultural attainment and commercial success in international markets was strongly asserted.

To assess the achievements of the *Werkbund* in its early years against the pronouncements of such an ambitious programme leads almost inevitably to the judgment that it failed. Despite calls for unity, the membership and its attitudes remained diverse and disparate. The belief in quality and its cultural value was a common element, but was capable of such variable interpretations from the many points of view it encompassed, that the *Werkbund* was characterized from the beginning by deep and fundamental disputes, which eventually became so bitter they almost tore the organization apart. The most apt description of the *Werkbund* was in fact a phrase quoted by Hermann Muthesius: 'an association of the most intimate enemies.'

Yet if lack of unity hampered the achievement of its overall aims as a group interest, diversity brought tremendous vitality, even passion, to its debates, raising questions of contemporary relevance that gave the *Werkbund* pre-eminence in questions of design, not only in Germany, but across the whole of Europe. In its theoretical discussions, it summarized a range of concerns related to the development of modern society; its influence on education in the widest sense was profound; and through the designs of practitioner members it set new standards of achievement.

Its theoretical achievement lies in the fundamental shift from a backward-looking emphasis on the crafts, the central thrust of English nineteenth century theory culminating in the Arts and Crafts movement, to an acceptance of industry and mechanization as a vital factor in contemporary culture, an argument strongly and persistently advocated by Friedrich Naumann and elaborated in aesthetic terms by Hermann Muthesius. Although function was a guiding principle for all Werkbund practitioners, there was a difference, as Sebastian Müller has pointed out, between those who thought of the functionalism of art and those emphasizing the artistic character of functionalism.[160] Muthesius' contribution was to clearly articulate the latter.

Throughout his writings he condemned the use of ornament to endow objects with artistic validity, dismissing the 'hot-house atmosphere' of rapidly changing stylistic fashions, culminating in *Jugendstil*, that 'has brought almost as great a confusion as the previously existent repetition of historic styles.'[161] For Muthesius, the concept of function required no superfluous 'artistic' cladding to have aesthetic value. Instead, *sachlichkeit*, or practicality, was the basis of a visual language capable of expressing contemporary cultural values. 'Appliances and equipment ... must also be regarded from the point of view of form, i.e., the effect they will have on the eye. This is principally the province of the engineer, who creates tools and machines to make work easier, and fashions bridges, railways, and vehicles for traffic, and weapons for war ... we admire a fine surgical instrument because of its elegance, a vehicle because of its pleasing lightness, a wrought-iron bridge soaring over a river because of its bold use of material. And we are right to do so, for in the muscularity of those slim parts we confirm the triumph of technology which has risen to the limits of mastery of material.'[162]

There was, however, no automatic equation between function and aesthetic value. For a work to have artistic effect it must embody artistic feeling. 'The idea that it is quite sufficient for the engineer designing a building, an appliance, a machine, merely to fulfil a purpose, is erroneous, and the recent often-repeated suggestion that if the object fulfils its purpose then it is beautiful as well is even more erroneous. Usefulness has basically nothing to do with beauty. Beauty is a problem of form, and nothing else; usefulness is the plain fulfilment of a purpose.'[163]

The dominant criterion in aesthetic judgment was therefore that of form, and central to Muthesius' theories was the inclusion of industrial practice, indeed of any aspect of human potential as creative form-giver: '...the whole of mankind's activity, in tool-making, in building, in construction design, in fact all his visible activites, is subject in a general sense to the same principle..., namely, the combining of the useful and the beautiful.'[164]

Muthesius totally rejected the view that technical and mechanical practice was irreconcilable to the artistic spirit, advocating instead that anything, from a sofa-cushion to a city-plan (Vom Sofakissen zum Städtebau), was capable of spiritual value, provided it embodied a sensitivity for form. 'Of far more importance than the material world is the spiritual; in other words, form stands higher than function, material and technology.'[165] A concern for form should therefore be intrinsic to all human creativity and could not be reduced to the dispensible addition of 'artistic' decoration, or solely given validity by artistic genius.

The primacy of form in Muthesius' aesthetic, therefore, could not be left to individual taste or inclination, which would simply result in the confusion of the past he so vehemently criticized being endlessly repeated. Instead, it was necessary to re-establish a unified German culture based on the social, material and economic conditions of the age, which was manifested in his concept of the 'type', of standardized forms. In this, he drew upon Semper's idea of basic forms and also looked to the English Arts and Crafts movement as an example, seeing in it a style based on indigenous traditions yet bearing the stamp of contemporaneity. It was one of the most crucial elements of his theory and probably the most controversial.

In architecture, Muthesius argued, a tradition had been handed down through history, embodying continuity, stability, a sense of eternal values, and individual striving for effect and ephemeral forms were alien to these values. 'Of all the arts, architecture tends towards the typical. Only in this can it find its consummation. Only through the universal and constant pursuance of this same purpose can the excellence and con-fident certainty be reconquered, that we admire in the achievements of past ages, marching a unified path.' His argument was not confined to architecture, however, but was further enlarged by his attitude to technological development, in which he saw a tendency for invention to find, over a period, typical forms most appropriate to their function.[166] Types therefore provided the basis for accepted cultural standards, which were necessary for the formation of a high-level of general taste amongst the public, giving a sense of certainty and reassurance. Muthesius agreed specifically with Langbehn that individuality was the essence of German creativity, but reconciled this to his concept of the type, also following Langbehn, by emphasizing German capacity for subordination to a greater ideal. Throughout his writings, in both imagery and terminology, there are clear implications of social as well as aesthetic aims: the ideal of a unified architecture and culture was represented as being synonymous with a unified, ordered society.

Muthesius' ideas can therefore be seen as corresponding in essential respects with those of Friedrich Naumann, though also considerably extending them with regard to the potential of art in relation to modern technology. Between them, these two men provided a theory corresponding in its main thrust to contemporary middle-class, liberal political ambitions. However, although emphasizing a unifed culture and society, it was not by any means a democratic concept.

This was demonstrated by Joseph August Lux, a foundation-member of the *Werkbund,* who in a range of publications drew upon many of the ideas of Muthesius and Naumann. In an article in *Innendekoration* published in 1908 under the title, 'The Artistic Problem of Industry', he began with the assertion: 'The artistic problem of our age does not lie in the arts and crafts, it lies in industry.' The crafts, he went on, expressed and served the needs of personality and were not for the masses, whose needs were satisfied by industry, which '. . . serves the masses. It emerged from the masses and is only justified by them.' Industry was incapable of producing art, which could only be created by the personal skill and spiritual inspiration of the artist. What Lux called 'an incredible falsification' resulted from the belief that industry could provide the masses with art, 'which they have never understood and will never understand.' This falsification could only end by industry 'serving good taste', producing articles that were 'purposeful, practical and beautiful'.

Lux therefore differed from Muthesius in rejecting the possibility of 'spiritual inspiration' in industrial products, and there was a further difference of emphasis when he considered the constraints on artists working in industry: 'Only the quality of the form is dependent upon the artist. The quality of workmanship and material are determined by other factors, that are not in his power.' The problem of industry was therefore the factor of quality, which was determined by social, economic and ethical powers beyond the control of artists. The latter had, if part of industry's technical leadership, the ability to broaden good taste through their designs and improve everyday standards. However: 'To make the masses artistic, is a hopeless business . . . The masses can only be made bearable, if their bad products are withheld and good exclusively provided. They need not be consulted, for they have no judgment. Large industry only has the power to determine the market and to alter the state of affairs in favour of culture.'[167]

Whereas Muthesius expressed an ideal of unity, which had a powerful intellectual coherence, Lux's views were a mixture of pragmatism and polemic. The latter, however, should not obscure his capacity to appreciate the significance of many underlying trends of his age. Although he rejected the possibility of machines producing art, in other articles he acknowledged the achievements of engineers as giving the age a stylistic stamp which differentiated it from all others, indirectly influencing all aspects of life. In this, he showed a breadth of appreciation absent in the more nationalist emphasis of many contemporary theorists, in his recognition of the influence of America. There, he said, 'Everything is based on reason, everything stems from the investigation of life and its requirements. Imagination has nothing to do with it.' This led him to castigate the *völkisch* artist, who emphasized imagination against reason and was 'an open or secret opponent of modernism . . . The modern artist, however, sets his reason against imagination, the sensibility of his nature allows him to comprehend the modern task more deeply and certainly than mastering the sentimentality of past art allows.'[168]

Lux's arguments attempted to draw an emphatic demarcation between the crafts and industry. He wanted to halt the decline of the former and assert its positive value in contemporary culture, hence his stress on the unique artistic potential of the crafts. The need for a clear differentiation led, in his analysis of industry and technology, to an acceptance of the real limitations confronting designers in industry. Whilst echoing Muthesius in recognizing the truly innovative aspects of modern technology in its capacity to produce standard products in large quantities at a consistently high level of quality, and stressing the general benefit that could accrue, the dimension of social idealism was absent from his writings, for he simply didn't believe in its possibilities. To characterize him as elitist or undemocratic is to state the obvious, though neither term adequately conveys the tone of arrogant contempt evident in some passages. If his views on the potential of artists in industry were realistic in avoiding the utopian expectations of many of his contemporaries, and indeed prophetic since he identified a pattern that has since become widely

Hermann Muthesius

Henry van der Velde.

apparent, his social attitudes revealed him as a prisoner of his class and time.

Lux's scepticism about the *Werkbund*'s declared aim of widespread cultural reform led to him resigning his membership in 1908. He had many views in common with one of the most influential economists of the age, Werner Sombart, who was also a member for a short time, from 1908 to 1910, and similarly dismissed any possibility of influencing the mass market. Sombart went further than Lux, however, in rejecting any possibility of artists having effective influence in industry under the capitalist system, which he saw as an expression of Western commercial and materialist values and a negation of German heroic idealism.

Such pessimism was untypical of the *Werkbund* membership, however, which generally took a much more positive approach to its declared aims, though it very soon became apparent that there were deep differences over how to achieve them. Once again, Muthesius found himself under attack.

Chief amongst his opponents was Henry van der Velde, who joined the *Werkbund* in 1908 and soon became a prominent figure in its activities. Van der Velde had played no direct part in the actual events preceding the establishment of the *Werkbund*, but his status as both practitioner and theorist gave him considerable influence. The emphasis on a more prominent role for artists culminating in the Dresden exhibition had been one of the vital forces in the coalition which led to the foundation of the organization, and it was for this tendency that van der Velde became the spokesman. His powerful advocacy of their cause was founded on strong convictions, but there was also an element of personal antagonism against Muthesius, who had repeatedly and disdainfully reflected the *Jugendstil* influences and individualism epitomized by van der Velde. Indeed, in both character and ideas, they represented a stark contrast.

Whereas Muthesius stressed the aesthetic potential of functional form, van der Velde inverted the argument, vehemently advancing the claims of art and its functional role. Although also writing admiringly of rational forms evolved by modern technology, his appreciation remained on an aesthetic level. There could be no unification of art and industry, he stated, for that would inevitably mean the subordination of art. Beauty and morality, the essence of art, were alien to the profit motive of industry, and for their realization a revolution was necessary, with industry converted to an ideal of art. To bring this about leading artists had to create the forms and ornament of a new style, corresponding to the ideas and needs of the age. By such means, artists could use industry to educate the public to an awareness of art and beauty as an integral part of their daily lives, and for those producing goods, realize Ruskin's definition that art stems from everything created in joy. Like Sombart, though from the standpoint of craft socialism in the Morrisian tradition, his opposition was not just to industrial production, but the economic system in which it was embedded. 'I would not be a modern man,' he proclaimed, 'if I did not seek to adapt the production of objects, that earlier originated from human hands and were prepared by artist-craftsmen, to the new kinds of mechanical and industrial manufacture.

But if it suits industry that we should henceforeward defend every kind of business, and the machine and mechanical production, so they will create in us the certainty not to sacrifice the idea of beautiful work and the idea of good quality of materials, which means in fact the morality of objects, to a transformation that would eventually only culminate in the enlargement of profits for the benefit of industrialists.'[169] Artists he added, had worked to enrich human culture since time immemorial, and no group had more right to speak of what would endanger or advance it. Van der Velde thus gave uncompromising expression to a belief in the priest-like function of artists as guardians of morality and human values, to which industry should be subordinate, an attitude hardly commending him to the industrial members.

Although the continual confrontation of van der Velde and Muthesius was the most dramatic aspects of *Werkbund* activities, a majority of leading figures eschewed radical theory and adopted a more conservative stance. The most influential figure in this respect was Paul Schultze-Naumburg, who advocated a traditionalism evolved in the context of the *Bund Heimatschutz*, emphasizing in particular, the *Biedermeier* period as a model of simple elegance, adaptable to modern conditions as a symbol of continuity. For others, such as Theodor Fischer and Richard Riemerschmid, a sense of continuity was equally important, though drawing inspiration from regional craft traditions. In fact, although most members accepted that the ideal of quality could be realised equally well by hand-tools or machines, a strong residual bias towards craft-culture was widely evident. Karl Schmidt's *Dresdener Werkstätten* was a model in this respect. The role designers played, the use of mechanization to sustain craft values, its consistently high product quality, and the later construction of a garden-city settlement to further the ideal of a working community, all gave it a special place in the *Werkbund*'s affairs.

The *Werkbund* was not just a debating

Ladies bedroom for the Westend house, Berlin, by Bruno Paul, 1909.

The firm of Oskar Winter of Hannover was well known for its cast-iron heating stoves which were smaller in scale than traditional tiled versions and thus more appropriate for small, modern apartments. The company also branched out into the production of gas cooking-hobs, as advertized here in a poster of 1903 by Wilhelm Schulz, and gas ovens. Separate units were still the norm and this hob would have been located on a kitchen table-top.

society, however, but an organization dedicated to practical improvement and a vital strand of its activities was a range of initiatives for educating the public to an awareness and sympathy with its aims, in which Karl-Ernst Osthaus played a prominent part. A banker's son from Hagen in Westphalia, he began a career there as commercial apprentice to a textile company. It was obviously an unhappy experience. He left after a nervous breakdown and, influenced by Langbehn's ideas, determined to commit himself to art and the cultural reform movement. On inheriting his grandparents' wealth he travelled widely, building a collection of works in North Africa and the Near East that later formed the basis of the Folkwang Museum, which he founded at Hagen in 1899. He organized an exhibition of crafts from his home town for the 1906 Dresden exhibition and joined the *Werkbund* in 1908, one of a large number of museum directors active in the organization.

Osthaus' distinctive contribution was to persuade the Werkbund to jointly finance a new musuem at Hagen, the *Deutsches Museum für Kunst in Handel und Gewerbe* (the German Museum for Art in Trade and Commerce), dedicated to propagating the new initiative. A large collection of contemporary artefacts and posters was assembled, supplemented by slides, photographs and documentation. To be effective, however, Osthaus realized it was necessary to reach out to a broad public. Hagen was therefore established as a base for travelling exhibitions, with a large number being rapidly mounted and despatched. A particular target was salesmen, who were to be enlisted as art educators to the public at large. Exhibitions such as *Die Kunst im Dienste des Kaufmann's* (Art in the service of the salesman) and a lecture series *Zur Geschmacksausbildung des deutschen Kaufmann's* (Towards educating the taste of the German salesman) were established to this end. Osthaus believed that

shop windows should be a street museum of modern art, (his initiatives led to the establishment of a course in window-decoration in Berlin) and ships, trains and railway stations used as sites for his concept of a mobile museum. Before long, exhibitions were being despatched internationally, twelve such by 1911, one of the most successful being a joint venture with the Austrian Museum for Art and Industry in Vienna, which toured the USA in 1912-13, arousing great interest. There was, however, some criticism of Osthaus within the *Werkbund* for what was viewed as an imbalanced emphasis on craft work in the collection and activities at Hagen, which was one more sign of the tensions in the organization.

Another enterprise to propagate Werkbund ideas was the publication of a yearbook, commencing in 1912. These were substantial bound volumes, containing articles, the texts of conference speeches and discussions, and a large selection of illustrations of members' work. The latter, in particular, gave a vivid insight into the great diversity of achievement and concept amongst the membership. The yearbooks were also significant in disseminating an awareness of the *Werkbund* and its activities, being easily disseminated by post.

A highly original initiative, undertaken jointly with the *Dürerbund* in 1913, was the preparation of a compendium of high quality domestic goods which represented value for money and had the cachet of approval by both organizations. A joint committee selected the objects and it was intended they should be featured in a nationwide chain of shops at the time of publication. The outbreak of war delayed publication until 1915, however, and the resultant *Deutsches Warenbuch* was not as successful as hoped. Nevertheless, the idea of a selection of goods exemplary in quality and price was later to be revived and developed on several occasions.

The annual conferences of the *Werkbund* also became notable events, receiving wide

Furniture for a
gentleman's study
designed by Walter
Gropius and illustrated in
the first *Werkbund*
yearbook, 1912.

Tea-service designed by
Henry van der Velde and
executed by Th. Müller of
Weimar, from the first
German *Werkbund*
yearbook of 1912.

Cover of the first yearbook of the German *Werkbund* published in 1912. The title can be translated as 'The Spiritualization of German Work'.

DIE DURCHGEISTIGUNG DER DEUTSCHEN ARBEIT

JAHRBUCH DES DEUTSCHEN WERKBUNDES 1912

Page from the *Deutsches Warenbuch* of 1915. The products it illustrated were considered exemplary in quality and price. On the left at the top is a portable electric cooker and travelling-iron complete with case. The lower illustration is of tea-making equipment.

M 154
Kocher und Bügeleisen, elektr., für die Reise, mit Koffer

M 155
Bügeleisen, elektr.

M 156
Wärmer

M 157
Heißwasserkanne

M 158
Kessel mit Kocher

M 159
Wärmer

Glasses and ceramic containers in holders for bathroom use, illustrated in the *Deutsches Warenbuch* of 1915.

publicity in newspapers and journals of all kinds. Held in major cities, Munich, Frankfurt, Berlin, Dresden and Vienna, they came to include exhibitions and events open to the public, as well as a social round that must have exhausted participants.

In the seven years of its existence before the First World War, the *Werkbund,* as a result of its educational and propaganda program-mes came to be regarded as the authoritative body on questions of design in Germany and was widely emulated in other countries. Its membership rose from 492 in 1908 to 1870 in 1914 and included most of the outstanding talent of the time. After a short period of existence and success, it seemed to many members that the time was ripe for a major event to publicize the *Werkbund* and firmly establish its position in national life.

The idea of a major exhibition to demon-strate the achievements and aims of the *Werkbund* was first mooted in its committee in 1911. Cologne was suggested as the site and Peter Behrens was asked to formulate pro-posals for an organizational framework. His plan, submitted in March 1912, had three main themes: firstly, workshops and displays showing the concept of quality in production; secondly, model shops showing the role of art and taste in presentation and trade pro-motion; thirdly, a review of exemplary prod-ucts to demonstrate the artistic achievements of the *Werkbund.* Behrens seems to have had in mind an approach similar to that adopted for the 1906 Dresden exhibition, with artists having the deciding role. The scale of the new proposal was so large, however, that com-mercial support was vital for its realization. For this reason Behrens' plan was not pursued, though the resultant compromise of what for many members constituted an im-portant point of principle was not adopted without opposition. Published early in 1913, the definitive programme by the Cologne City Architect, Carl Rehorst, sought to group ex-hibits under thematic heads, but in order to fill

the large site and ensure financial viability, exhibits by commercial and regional organiz-ations were included. Inevitably the result was that the effect of the exhibition was more diffused than those members who wanted to strictly emphasize the quality concept would have wished. Even amongst the exhibits of leading *Werkbund* members considerable variety was evident.

Probably the clearest evidence of this were the major buildings erected for the event. Behrens' Festival Hall, Josef Hoffmann's Austrian Pavilion and Muthesius' pavilion for the Hamburg-Amerika Line all revealed a stripped Neo-classical style derived from the *Biedermeier* period which was beginning to enjoy considerable vogue. Henry van der Velde's theatre, however, was a *Jugendstill* derivative, its curving organic lines attempting to integrate both exterior and interior elements into a whole, but never succeeding entirely in overcoming the basic, rectangular construc-tional features. Walter Gropius, a promising young architect, who had gained a reputation for industrial buildings, designed a model factory which showed a daring use of glazed elements, though the structure remained founded on the Neo-classical principles Gropius had absorbed whilst a pupil of Behrens. Another young architect, Bruno Taut, created a small pavilion from glass-bricks, glazed tiles and mosaics intended as a demonstration piece for the material, which used coloured elements and the play of light to stunning effect. In addition, and often over-looked in the *post-hoc* process of selecting what was significant, were a wide range of historical and regional forms. The Bremen-Oldenburg House had a dining-room by Paul Ludwig Troost in Neo-Baroque style with in-tricate plaster work and decorative items. Runge and Scotland also had a room with marble-topped tables, carved chairs and elaborately decorated wallpaper, carpet and fabrics. Wilhelm Lossow and Max Kühne sought to give a regional identity to the Saxon

Summerhouses designed
by Max Heidrich for the
Berhard Stadler
workshops at Paderborn.
Shown at the Werkbund
Exhibition, Cologne,
1914.

Cafe-Restaurant in the
Bremen-Oldenburg
pavilion at the 1914
Werkbund Exhibition in
Cologne. It was
designed by the Bremen
partnership of Runge and
Scotland.

Interior of the Hamburg-
Amerika pavilion by
Hermann Muthesius for
the 1914 *Werkbund*
Exhibition. Although
Muthesius' theories were
advanced, his practical
designs at this time
tended to fall into the
pattern of simplified
Neo-classicism that had
become popular since
the turn of the century.

132

Hall designed by Walter Gropius for Hermann Gerson of Berlin and exhibited in the interior design section of the 1914 *Werkbund* exhibition. Gropius' furniture and interiors of this period were heavy and conventional compared with his major architectural designs, such as the model factory constructed at Cologne for the exhibition.

Serving-counter on a railway dining-car designed by August Endell for Van der Zypen & Charlier of Cologne. Both the kitchen and serving-section had built-in furniture and continuous working-surfaces that later became a standard feature of kitchen design.

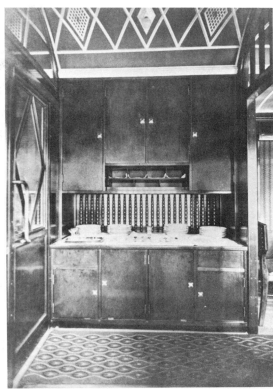

Tea- and coffee-set in stoneware designed by Hermann Haas for Villeroy & Boch and exhibited at the 1914 *Werkbund* exhibition.

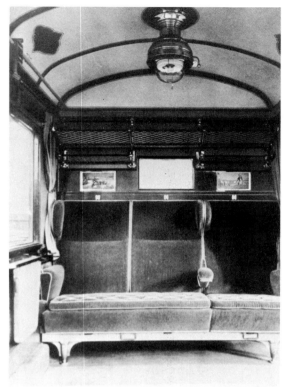

The Transport Hall at the 1914 *Werkbund* Exhibition. The single-deck tramcars behind the locomotive were designed by E. Aberle for Gustav Talbot & Cie of Aachen.

Second-class passenger compartment designed by Rudolf Rochga for Würtemburg State Railways and executed in their Cannstadt workshops. Shown at the 1914 *Werkbund* Exhibition.

Railway dining-car interior by August Endell for Van der Zypen & Charlier, shown at the 1914 *Werkbund* Exhibition.

House, using local craftsmen to create items such as large wrought-iron gates and screens.

There were also a series of rooms in which individual artists could display complete furnishings or a selection of their work. Bruno Paul's furniture on this occasion was made by the Berlin firm of Hermann Gerson but remained in his refined version of the *Biedermeier* style. Gerson also made three suites to the designs of Walter Gropius that equally displayed early nineteenth century influences in their solid forms, rich materials and sparingly decorated panels. Max Heidrich and Bernhard Stadler of the Paderborn Workshops designed a summer-house with heavily-upholstered furniture, repetitive patterns on surfaces and heavily-draped curtains. The *Deutsche Werkstätten* had up-market products from their leading designers, Riemerschmid, Niemayer and Bertsch, but also a lush room with draped bed in Empire Style by Lucien Bernhard. Whilst Pankok and van der Velde continued with the curvilinear furniture derived from *Jugendstill*, Behrens displayed Neo-classical furnishings for the German Embassy in Leningrad, of which he was architect.

The pattern of diversity was repeated in the smaller exhibits, ranging from traditional forms of stoneware in the ceramics section through to a range of railway carriage interiors. The latter included a sleeping-carriage compartment by Gropius and a dining-car by August Endell, both for the Cologne company of Van der Zypen and Charlier, and a third-class carriage by Oswin Hempel for the *Sächsischen Waggon-Fabrik* at Werdau.

The great variety of forms demonstrated the extent to which *Werkbund* members had succeeded in gaining commissions, often in new fields of activity. At the same time, however, it was abundantly clear that the formal unity so often declared as an aim of the cultural reform movement, was as far away as ever.

Whilst the exhibits stood as evidence of divergences in practice, the annual conference of the *Werkbund*, which opened on July 5th in Behrens Festival Hall, saw the accumulated theoretical tensions behind that diversity explode into impassioned conflict.

The detonator was a key-note address by Hermann Muthesius on 'The *Werkbund*'s Tasks of the Future'. His central theme was the concept of *Typisierung*, or standards of good form and good taste, evidence of which he saw emerging in recent years and believed should be broadened amongst both producers and consumers. The establishment of domestic cultural standards could then serve as a platform for world exports and the diffusion of German culture abroad. Essentially it was a summary of ideas expounded over the previous decade.

Prior to the conference, Muthesius had circulated ten theses that were the basis of his speech, but realizing that opposition had been aroused, his full text was less polemical in tone. Immediately he finished speaking, however, Henry van der Velde took the floor and read out a list, compiled the night before with several supporters, of ten counter-theses. These vehemently asserted the freedom of the artists, branded *Typisierung* as a restriction of that freedom, and rejected the subordination of art to commercial policy. Quality, claimed van der Velde, was created for a limited group of patrons and connoisseurs, and only through such patronage could artists create style, which had not yet emerged, but was a precondition of any concept of *Typisierung*.

On the surface, this confrontation was one of ideas, but underlying it were longstanding conflicts of personality and policy. The views expressed by both main protagonists were not new, had been publicly expressed for many years, and were, in fact, part of a common currency of debate. In addition, there was also obvious at Cologne an accumulated resentment against the decisions leading to the commercialization of the 1914 exhibition, and pique at the allocation of space and building commissions associated with it. Of greatest significance and what emerged most clearly, however, in the debate on the day following Muthesius' speech and in subsequent manoeuvrings, was not just a continuation of earlier differences but a bid to assume leadership in the *Werkbund* by a group of *avant-garde* artists and their sympathizers, which together with van der Velde, included Walter Gropius, one of the most vehement opponents of Muthesius, K.-E. Osthaus, Bruno Taut, Hans Poelzig and August Endell. At the root of the attempt was a deep dissatisfaction with the entire direction of *Werkbund* policy and by seizing control, it was hoped to decisively assert the claims of artists, even if it meant splitting the organization.

Hermann Muthesius epitomized their dissatisfaction. It is often overlooked that he was an official in the Prussian Ministry of Commerce and therefore heir to the tradition of bureaucratic manipulation of society and economy for dynastic ends. This is not to suggest that Muthesius was simply a puppet of officialdom. He was a man of great conviction and achievement, both as an architect and administrator, but it was hardly a coincidence, that given his position, his views on matters such as cultural unity as a mirror of social unity, Germany's role in the world and the importance of trade in furthering it, were precisely in accordance with the overall trend of government policy. In fact, it would have been impossible for Muthesius as a civil servant to play the public role he did, had this not been the case. There were genuine aesthetic differences of opinion between Muthesius and van der Velde, as with the question of a new style. The former believed it already existed in embryo and required nourishing and diffusing; the latter asserted it had not yet emerged, and would only do so as a general quality perceptible in individual artistic striving. Underlying such differences, however, was a rejection of any idea that artists should play a

role subservient to state or commercial policy, and it is this that accounts for the passionate defence of individual, artistic autonomy expressed at the Cologne conference.

To many contemporary observers, the confrontation was no surprise. Robert Breuer wrote: 'That it would sometime or other have to come to an altercation between the different and often all-too-different groups and identities that have found themselves in the German *Werkbund*, less from inner need than on grounds of external politics, was obvious to every initiate. Sooner or later, the individualists, who recognize only their own daemon and nothing else in the world, would have to come to blows with the diplomats of the type...[170]

At the time, it seemed that van der Velde and his group had gained victory when Muthesius withdrew his theses. Further attempts to force his resignation, led by Gropius, failed however, the overwhelming majority of the membership wanting to preserve the organization's unity, fragile though it was, since it appeared that affairs of greater moment lay ahead. These events of the summer of 1914 became completely overshadowed by the outbreak of war in August. Little was achieved of lasting note and the very different circumstances prevailing at the end of the conflict were to alter The Werkbund's character and role in many important respects.

12 Ideal and Reality

Throughout its long and complex development, the cultural reform movement had articulated an extensive critique of contemporary design standards as a reflection of the economic and social structures and attitudes that produced them, proposing instead aesthetic programmes requiring, and in some respects intended to result in, an alternative social structure. If the culmination of those endeavours in the German *Werkbund* demonstrated many notable achievements, these were limited in scale and scope, and revealed the extent to which it was necessary to compromise when confronting realities which did not readily conform to theoretical preconceptions. It had been apparent in the work of the *Deutsche* and *Vereinigte Werkstätten* for the great shipping lines, where design idealism was confronted by the expectations of customers for an image corresponding to social status. It was also apparent in what at the time was regarded as a great breakthrough for the cultural reform movement, in the work of Peter Behrens for the giant electrical firm, AEG.

Behrens' appointment to AEG in fact preceded the foundation of the *Werkbund*, so his work cannot be seen as a direct outcome of that body's activities. In his attitudes and achievement, however, he was very much a product of the same cultural initiatives leading to the *Werkbund's* foundation, and it was therefore hardly surprising that his role at AEG was regarded by many members as the realization of an ideal.

During the early years of the new century, Behrens had established himself amongst the front rank of German designers. Although much of his work continued to be for craft production, by 1905-6 he was executing commissions for the *Delmenhorster Linoleum Fabrik*, and exhibitions and advertising material for AEG. Though deriving from the

Peter Behrens.

Two arc-lamps for AEG designed by Peter Behrens, 1907-8.

earlier practice of commissioning artists for important projects, his appointment as artistic advisor to AEG in June, 1907 represented a new phase in company policy, stimulated by new production techniques and marketing concepts.

In Michael von Dolivo-Dobrowolsky, AEG had an outstanding production-engineer, who realized in the early years of the century that mass-production was most effective when concentrated not on specific artefacts, but the mechanized manufacture of high-quality standardized components usable in a wide variety of products. For him, an artefact was thus a solution to a technical problem, an assemblage of components, and he paid little attention to external form.

The importance of the latter was appreciated, however, by Paul Jordans, AEG's technical director. He was probably responsible for appointing Behrens, who later recalled him saying: 'Do not believe that even an engineer, if he buys a motor, takes it apart in order to investigate it. He too as an expert buys according to the external impression. A motor must look like a birthday present.'[171]

Behrens' role as artistic director therefore differed substantially from the limited and occasional commissions previously given to architects and artists. His was a permanent appointment with complete control over all visual aspects of AEGs installation, products and publications. It signified a new awareness in the company of the importance of product appearance as a competitive weapon in world markets, and Behrens' work for AEG was remarkable for the time in its range and diversity.

The first evidence of it were products and graphic items, the building he designed being on a scale involving a longer time-span. In 1907-8, for example, he worked on the large carbon-arc lamps constituting the main form of lighting in production, (though in the process of being made obsolete by filament bulbs). His changes were simple but effective,

Two humidifiers and an electric clock designed by Peter Behrens for AEG, c.1910. Behrens also designed the type-face used for the clock numerals.

Electric kettles designed by Peter Behrens for AEG in 1909. The three basic forms, cylinder, half-circle and octagonal are illustrated.

replacing a dull matt-black finish with olive green, still serviceable but giving a lighter feel. The lamps were balanced compositions of volumes, highlighted by brass beading, screws and chains. A clean, distinctive appearance was achieved by meticulous attention to colour, materials and form, an approach evident in other products, such as overhead and table fans, electric clocks and instrument panels.

Dolivo-Dobrowolsky's component-standardization was most apparent in a range of electric kettles dating from 1909. Three basic forms were designed, cylindrical, half-oval and octagonal, each in three sizes, 0.75, 1.25 and 1.75 litre capacity. All were produced in

Domestic heater by Peter Behrens for AEG c.1907-8, manufactured from hammered metal sheet. It is a composition of geometrical motifs which Behrens believed appropriate for the decoration of functional objects.

brass, which could optionally be nickel or copper plated, thus giving three material finishes. To these, three surface treatments were specified: plain, hammered or straked. Items such as plugs, elements, handles and knobs were similarly produced to standard patterns. Potentially, there were 81 possible variations, though only 30 were marketed.

Behrens' appointment caused some surprise. The journal *Deutsche Kunst und Dekoration*, in an article on him, commented: 'The name Behrens means an artistic programme, a highly individual direction in art, which does not know compromise. Certainly Behrens stands out as a recognized force, but from the beginning he was stamped by a bristling, intransigent manner. Why should one choose him, this most resolute formalist?' The article concluded AEG was now of such a size and importance that: 'Artistically given form should symbolically express the power, significance and dignity of the whole undertaking.'[172] If that judgement is accurate, and there is much to substantiate it, Behrens' work for AEG anticipated the modern concept of corporate identity, and indeed, a modern practitioner in this field, Wally Olins, has identified him as a forerunner.[173]

Behrens frequently expounded his own concept of the role he played in the company. In a lecture given in association with an exhibition of his early work for AEG in 1909, he stated the objects on display were not 'so-called applied art products, but objects of use, that serve less to decorate the human environment and above all have to service a useful purpose.' This distinction has echoes of the standpoint of Joseph August Lux. The emphasis, said Behrens, was on 'good proportions' rather than ornament, but where the latter was necessary or desirable it should be impersonal, which was best expressed in geometric forms.

It is worth noting that Behrens did not eschew decoration, but felt it should be 'impersonal' and 'geometrical'. In practice, there was a clear division in the products he designed for AEG, those for industrial use being plain and functional, but for a domestic setting, decorative casings and finishes were the norm, as on his heaters and kettles. In short, his approach was modified to conform to differing market concepts and again, the predelictions of purchasers regarding the status of objects in a domestic environment.

There was a wider purpose to his work, however, expressed in the argument that modern manufacture made it possible 'to place a sophisticated technology in the service of culture. Through the mass-production of objects of use, corresponding to an aesthetically refined order, it is possible to carry taste into the broadest sections of the population.'[174] This was typical of the mainstream of argument amongst cultural reformers about their ideal role.

The current concept of raising general levels of taste and of the artist as preserver and progenitor of its values was therefore a consistent feature of his writings. The improvement of taste was necessary, argued Behrens, to facilitate the translation of creative work into material value and realize its economic benefits. This was linked to Germany's role in the world: 'In the final analysis, a culture of taste pervading a whole nation is witness to the activity of a nation.'[175]

In realizing the new culture, however, the relationship between art and technology was crucial, and he developed this theme in another lecture in 1910. Technology had resulted in the most impressive expressions of contemporary civilization, 'but not, at least not yet, a culture, if with H. St. Chamberlain, we understand civilization as all progress won through reason and enlightenment in material life, and under culture, the mental and spiritual values created through ideology and art.'[176] The problem for the age, despite many advances, was the separation of art and technology, which prevented the formal unity that was 'simultaneously the condition and proof of a style.' Though engineers might achieve results having aesthetic value, the fulfilment of functional and material purposes could not create art. The influential theories of Gottfried Semper which sought to derive artistic value from functional purpose and technology were condemned as 'an erroneous aesthetic' and 'a dogma of materialistic metaphysics.' Against that, Behrens argued: 'Art only originates from the intuition of strong individual characteristics and is the free fulfilment of psychic drives unhindered by material conditions.' The laws of technology, he went on, do not determine form, there is always the possibility of choice, and in that lies the possibility of beauty. Beauty and aesthetic value could be realized through the means of technology, but only if it were the instrument of artistic creativity: 'A mature culture,' he concluded, 'speaks only the language of art.'[177]

This standpoint had many similarities with the views of Henry van der Velde, who had indeed been a great influence on Behrens in his earlier *Jugenstil* phase, though there was one essential difference. Van der Velde's emphasis on the role of art in creating a sense of joy in work is missing from Behrens' statements. If one considers the history of AEG's labour relations at this time, however, that is hardly surprising. In 1907 its Berlin factories were heavily hit by strike action and it would have been illusory to pretend that improvements in design could solve labour problems of such dimensions. Behrens evaded this problem, concentrating on a lofty emphasis of art's potential in raising cultural standards through the interaction of enlightened manufacturer and consumer, which omitted the production stage, and any attempts to influence working procedures and attitudes.

Behrens did later design workers' housing for AEG, and also in 1912 a set of 'workers furniture' for a trade-union commission set up in Berlin to provide models for their members' homes. His attitude remained an autocratic one, however, based on a concept of reform handed down from above. In this, of course, he was not alone. The diaries for 1911/12 of Walther Rathenau, son of the founder of AEG, show that Behrens was a luncheon guest at his home, along with sucher figures as Werner Sombart, the art-historian Heinrich Wölfflin and the sculptor Georg Kolbe. Rathenau was also on close terms with Alfred Lichtwark and Theodor Fischer. Otto Eckmann and his wife, however, seemed to be particular friends, there being numerous mutual visits for lunch and tea.[178] The impression is that Behrens and Eckmann, amongst others, were very much at home in Berlin society. This is perhaps an indication of how far the young rebels of the 1890s had come in the intervening years, but there was obviously a price to be paid in accommodating to their more elevated status. There is no evidence, however, that either Behrens or Eckmann regretted the compromising of their ideals in return for a more effective, if acquiescent, role.

In general, however, in the years before the First World War, there was a trend away from an emphasis on art as a universal panacea, towards more modest aspirations. Anton Jaumann wrote in 1907 that fine art might once again play a role in the life of the nation, but the national economy could do without it at present without injury. To ignore applied art, he continued, was to deceive oneself about the essential basis of the economy, since 'A good part of the general welfare depends on the development of applied art.' As a nation dependent upon imports of raw materials and dependent upon exports, there was no future for Germay as a cheap mass-producer. 'If we are able to deliver such excellent goods that no people in the world can imitate them, then we have a winning hand.' The achievement of such standards would enable low cost work by unskilled workers to be left to other nations. To achieve quality, however, required that a sense for it should be created at home. 'The production of trashy goods ruins the workers. Like bad wages. The saving on wages is a thoroughly unproductive saving. Who pays low, has to regret poor treatment of materials by the workers ... Poor wages cause poor goods. ... With cheap, poor goods we ruin above all our international business, for nothing injures the sales-reputation of a nation so much as the label: cheap and nasty.'[179]

Just as the English emphasis on the crafts had been modified with the acceptance of mechanization, so Jaumann's views changed the emphasis on workers' creative fulfilment to a more limited concept of welfare in pursuit of quality in international competition.

The fact that Jaumann wrote regularly in Alexander Koch's journals, which at one time lyrically applauded the aristocratic patronage and exotic refinements of the Darmstadt colony, was in itself an indication of how attitudes had changed within the first decade of the century and it was part of a recurrent pattern. In 1909, Paul Westheim wrote an article on 'The Social Responsibility of Applied Art' which emphasized that all commercial work was based on social necessities. These were shaped by laws more powerful than individualism. 'Functionalism, usability and practicality are demanded of commercial objects.' Visual quality could give pleasure, 'but a procedure that seeks only to enjoy or judge objects of use in terms of visual value, will always grope around the kernel of the problem.' Such an approach could only be considered to be of secondary value, concluded Westheim, if individual work was preferred to an expression of social relationships in its context.[180]

A similar change was evident in Ferdinand Avenarius' journal Kunstwart, which also began to question the validity of 'life as a work of art', emphasizing instead qualities of comfort and usefulness. 'Out of aesthetic culture we have made a snob culture. It may perhaps be very high-minded, very stylish, but it is possible that because of it we starve.'[181]

The need to come to terms with the social and economic realities of the time was widely felt, and led to considerable divisions in the reform movement as a whole. For those advocating a less utopian programme than that demanded by the artists' faction, it seemed necessary to come to terms with a flood of new inventions and innovations which were becoming available and accessible. These, rather than the work of the cultural reformers, would seem to have provided the main visual stimulus and interest for the general public, and the scale on which they spread signalled a profound change in the material conditions of life. Although the possibility of personal possession of most of these innovations was a distant aspiration, access for a wider section of the population was increasingly available though public facilities. Simply the existence of many of these innovations, however, created enormous public curiosity and

A dining-room designed by Karl Bertsch for the Deutsche Werkstätten of Munich c.1913, from a watercolour by Wilhelm Volz. Bertsch's forms were always simple, but strong and clearly articulated, often using an emphatic contrast of colours, such as the dark tones of the dining suite and the green leather upholstery.

Showroom designed by Theodor Veil of Munich, c.1912, for the exhibition 'Women in Art and Fashion', held at Hermann Hirschwald's gallery, the Hohenzollern-Kunstgewerbehaus in Berlin. The employment of a designer to create settings appropriate for each exhibition was yet another indication of Hirschwald's continuing commitment to bringing what he considered the best of contemporary applied art to Berlin over a period of thirty years.

An early Zeppelin over central Berlin. The type is unidentified but is possibly the LZ3 of 1908. These remarkable designs of Graf von Zeppelin were amongst the most dramatic sights of the age, exciting enormous public interest. Their rigid construction to contain the flexible helium/hydrogen gas bags was based on a revolutionary use of a modular aluminium frame.

interest.

Perhaps the most exciting, though for most people, the most remote development, was the realization of the age-old dream of powered flight, which was progressing beyond early, tentative experiments into a more assured phase. At the time, the greatest attention focussed on rigid airships, in the design and construction of which Germany was a world leader, largely due to the work of Graf Zeppelin. The huge, cigar-shaped forms cruising across the sky seemed a pointer to the future, particularly when compared to the

comparatively flimsy nature and limited capacity of aircraft. Their shapes were still strongly influenced by observations from nature, as with the Rumpler *Taube* (Pigeon), which although having a strikingly innovative monoplane wing-construction, was imitative in its trailing edges of bird wings. Wooden frame construction covered with stretched canvas was the predominant technique employed, giving fuselages a box-like cross-section, though some early experiments with welded tubular-steel frames indicated the possibilities of other structural forms, and by

145

The Rumpler *Taube* monoplane aircraft of 1910 was based on Louis Bleriot's aircraft that first flew the Channel. It was typical of much early aircraft design in following natural forms.

An early example of heavy goods vehicle construction by Daimler, capable of carrying 5000 kg. Such vehicles were beginning to oust horse-drawn transport in the early years of the century.

A Siemens-Halske experimental electric locomotive of 1906 with angled front surfaces to reduce wind resistance.

Motor-cycles such as this *Brennabor* model of c.1910 marked a significant advance in powered personal transportation over pedal-cycles, though its form was still based on the bicycle diamond frame.

Interior cab of the Siemens-Halske electric locomotive of 1906. The layout with the large steering wheels is similar to contemporary airship practice.

Express locomotive built in 1904 by Henschel for Prussian State Railways. The streamlined cladding and the cab situated at the front of the engine, rather than behind the boiler, were radical changes from conventional practice.

Gas water-heater used in a model gas kitchen designed by Rudolf and Fia Wille in 1906. Such appliances made a constant supply of hot water readily available in domestic homes of all kinds for the first time. (courtesy: RIBA)

A gas-stove of 1906, the Askania Model III, which followed the general practice of the time in having a separate burner range and oven at table-top level. Decorative mouldings were still considered an important selling-point for domestic appliances.

1912 the firm of Junkers was developing an all metal 'plane that later became its hallmark.

On the roads motor-vehicles were becoming commonplace. Both mechanical parts and bodywork were heavily dependent upon craft skills and the consequent high cost limited ownership of personal vehicles. However, omnibus services and commercial freight vehicles were growing steadily in number and changing the urban street scene. For most of the public, a bicycle was economically within their reach and transformed personal mobility, giving a greater range of possibilities for work, residence and leisure, with cycle-racing becoming a popular sport.

Electric tramways probably made the greatest difference in cities, however, providing frequent and reliable services over short distances. The most dramatic indicator of the potential of electric traction, however, was provided on an experimental stretch of electrified line on a military railway between Marienfeld and Zossen, when in 1903 an electric locomotive reached a speed of 130mph. The influence of this achievement was manifested in 1906 in a new drive-unit for the track by Siemens-Halske, which had a pointed form at the ends in order to reduce air-resistance as far as possible. This early attempt at streamlining was described as making 'a somewhat adventurous impression.'

The concept of streamlining had a long and complex evolution stemming from nineteenth century studies in the natural sciences of the efficiency of fish-, animal- and bird-forms, though by the early twentieth century, visual concepts were becoming abstracted from natural forms. In 1904, the firm of Henschel produced an express locomotive in streamlined cladding for Prussian State Railways. Less dramatic, but in practice more successful, from 1908 onwards, Maffei of Munich produced a series of express passenger locomotives for Bavarian State Railways, with a conical boiler door and protruding features

swept back. They were widely regarded, both visually and in terms of performance, as amongst the finest designs of their time.

In the field of information communication, telegraph and radio enabled news to be rapidly sent around the world, but in this context, the breakthrough most accessible to the public was the telephone. Services had grown since the 1880s, but in 1912 Siemens introduced a coin-operated, direct-dialling public telephone that gradually spread across the country.

Although other forms of power were important, the greatest expansion was in electricity. AEG were not the only company in this field, and the provision of power together with the refinement of the small electric motor brought an increasing range of appliances to the market, irons, cooking-rings and ovens, heaters and kettles, vacuum cleaners, polishers and hair-dryers, amongst others. Many were initially intended for commercial use, but gradually made inroads into the domestic markets in the first decade of the century. Electric lighting had already transformed street illumination, work-places and shops, and it was also in the form of light-fittings that it spread in the home as simpler and inexpensive components became available.

The potential of electrical power in combination with other developments in public medicine, sanitation and housing, to contribute to a clean, easily maintained home, was also an important element in the contemporary stress on hygiene. 'Dust is the debris of human life-processes', thundered an author on the subject of hygiene in the home, '...the enemy must be fought with stronger weapons, as demonstrated by the great discovery of the new age, the vacuum cleaning apparatus, as it were, the modern quick-firing gun in this struggle.'[182]

Science, technology and industry were vaunted by some, feared by others, but no aspect of life or consciousness remained un-

Award-winning school desks produced by A.W. Remy & Cie of Neuwied c.1901. The seat form was designed to correspond exactly to the body form of pupils and in its concern for adequate space for cleaning, comfortable working position and healthy posture, this desk anticipated many of the essential concerns of later designers, reaching far beyond questions of style.

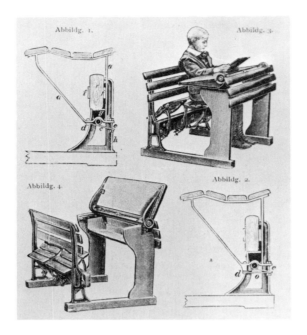

touched by them. The scale of their impact was such that the reform movement in applied art could not ignore them, if it wished to have any real role or significance in modern life. Conceptually, this meant progressing beyond a superficial appreciation of 'technical form' or 'machine aesthetics', and adapting to commercial attitudes and procedures that represented a fundamental challenge to existing notions of applied art.

13 The First World War

In common with the populations of all the major combatant countries, the people of Germany saw the outbreak of war as the opening of a great heroic adventure which would unite the nation. On 4th August, Wilhelm II proclaimed a *Burgfrieden*, a civic truce, with his famous words, 'I no longer recognize parties; I recognize only Germans.' On the same day, the *Reichstag*, including the Social Democrats, voted to approve the war credits requested by the government. Cheering crowds accompanied the departure of the first of the two million troops under mobilization as they left for the fronts.

By November, however, the mood began to change. If any one turning point can be identified, it was a battle at Langemarck in Flanders, when in an effort to turn the flank of the British and French armies, four corps of young volunteers, idealistic but inadequately trained, were committed from reserve. They advanced singing a military song of their willingness to die for the Fatherland, and most did just that, cut to pieces in the concentrated fire of the professional infantry against which they had been pitted.

It soon became obvious that the war was not to be the short, glorious adventure originally envisaged, but a grim, bitter struggle. As it developed into the first total war in a modern sense, requiring the commitment of every human and material resource, the pressures and demands of the First World War accelerated change in every aspect of industry and society. The concentration of manufacture on military procurements meant a rapid diminution of luxury or inessential production, with a profound effect on the economic structure and manufacturing techniques of long-term significance. The sheer scale of material demands led to an even greater concentration of German industry into larger units, with a corresponding reduction of craft businesses, and an emphasis on mass-production.

The provision of adequate materials for the war effort immediately became an urgent concern. When in August 1914, Walther Rathenau learnt there was no policy for the rational allocation of strategic materials, he persuaded the War Ministry to establish a body to ascertain the level of stocks and control their distribution. A War Raw Materials Section was established in the ministry, directed by Rathenau and some of his AEG managers, to which representatives of other industries were added. This established a number of private corporations to buy, store and distribute materials, subject to government policy. This formula of self-administration in co-operation with government, was a classic example of a pattern established over many years in the Second Empire. In this case, only large companies could afford to invest in the raw materials corporations, and benefitted accordingly at the expense of smaller producers. Rathenau's initiative, however, together with the efforts of the German chemical industry to provide substitutes for essential imports cut off by the British naval blockade, ensured, for a time at least, an adequate flow of materials.

A further tendency towards centralization emerged from the demands of the military, as in the Franco-Prussian War, for greater standardization of war products. As in most combatant countries, the German military had remained strangely unaware of the potential of modern technology in war and the rapid expansion of production, particularly of mechanized equipment, revealed constant disparities between the same type of equipment produced by different companies. Prior to the war, the Society of German Engineers had promoted the standardization of materials and structural components, and many companies had introduced their own internal system of standards. As it became clearer that the war was 'no longer of man against man but of machine against machine'[183], urgent action became necessary. Therefore in 1916, the Chief of the War Office, General Groener, established the *Fabrikations-bureau* (Manufacturing Office) at Spandau near Berlin, which was a section to develop standardized specifications for military procurement. The director of this office, Chief Engineer Schachterle realized, however, that a more wide-ranging national organization was required. In December 1917, the *Normenausschuss der deutschen Industrie* (Standards Commission of Germany Industry) was established for this purpose, with representatives of government and industry grouped in committees for specific areas of concern. The influence of this body continued long after the end of the war.

The nationalist fervour and the focusing of all efforts on the needs of the war was also evident in the applied arts. The *Werkbund* yearbook of 1916 was dedicated, at Muthesius' suggestion, to the subject of war graves and memorials, and the organization mounted exhibitions which were consciously propagandistic, in neighbouring neutral countries.

The war was also seen as an opportunity to finally break any possible foreign influence on German culture. On its outbreak Henry van der Velde was hounded from his post at Weimar as an 'enemy alien'. In 1915, very much in the style of the time, Wilhelm von Bode wrote of Germany being engaged in a struggle against an alliance which had 'the furies of revenge, envy and barbarism inscribed upon their banners.' Only victory could secure Germany's cultural achievements, and justify its immeasurable sacrifices and Bode expressed the hope that the war would overcome 'the general levelling and decadence' and lead to 'a healthy, cleansing effect on the moral strengths of our nation.'[184]

In the same year, Hermann Muthesius also looked to victory 'to attain German form', and give the world an image by flooding it with German goods and wares.[185]

A means by which national identify could be confirmed was the use of domestic materials. When considering the outlook for quality products, Karl Schmidt pointed out in 1918 that reductions in raw material stocks could be beneficial, leading to an economical use of available supplies and, by fully utilizing indigenous timber, reduce the amount of imports to the benefit of the national trade-balance. He envisaged it would take several years in peacetime to satisfy the demand for furniture built-up in the war years, but saw that task as contributing to the evolution of a German style. This would express the national unity and consciousness strengthened in many Germans by the war, and would also have export potential in neighbouring countries. Even at this late stage, Schmidt spoke of the end of the war in a manner in which no consciousness was evident that defeat lay months away.

That people could not foresee catastrophe looming over the horizon is entirely understandable, but neither was there evident any sign of understanding that the war was bringing about fundamental change. In 1917 the Central Institute for Education in Berlin organized a series of lectures on the subject of 'Technology and Education'. Both Hermann Muthesius and Peter Behrens were guest speakers and each provided what was essentially a restatement of views formulated a decade earlier. Possibly as a concession to an audience of technologists they both clearly identified the role of mechanization in promoting comfort and well-being, before beating a well-trodden path in emphasizing cultural values as an instrument of national identity.

In contrast, for Heinrich Tessenow, an architect prominently involved in the Hellerau Garden City, the war represented the ultimate expression of the degeneration of industrial society and capitalism. What was needed, he argued, was the whole man, represented by the craftsman, in a social environment which could endow and sustain human values, namely the small town. For Tessenow also, the war provided an opportunity to re-emphasize a standpoint formed in the pre-war years.

As suffering and privation increased during the war, there was apparent some realization that fundamental change was needed to prevent such an event ever happening again, though actual opposition to the war was very limited. Bruno Taut envisaged architecture as the instrument of social redemption, creating structures in glass, the symbol of truthfulness and liberation, that would express the will of the people, uniting them one to another and with the cosmos — with architects replacing politicians as the saviours of society and morality.

Both Tessenow's craft society of wholeness and integrity, and the ecstatic mysticism of Taut's architect as leader, were incapable of realization, as was the assumption of Schmidt, Muthesius and Behrens, that life before the war would recommence much as before, when peace came. Both kinds of expectation was being undermined by changes taking place through the war.

The structure of industry and pace of technical development underwent a catalytic transformation in the forcing ground of the conflict. Motor vehicles, aircraft, airships and submarines became major instruments of strategy, with enormous resources poured into a period of concentrated development. Power sources, materials and production technology were equally subject to enormous change, as was the structure and organization of production. The monstrous demands of the war for ever greater quantities of every resource left no part of the German industrial economy untouched.

Facts and figures can be advanced to indicate the nature and proportions of such quantifiable changes. Less tangible, but perhaps more profound, was the way industrial products altered the whole concept of war. What began as an heroic test of manhood rapidly deteriorated into appalling butchery in the slaughter of battlefields such as the Somme and Verdun. The dehumanizing impact and sense of utter insignificance under the monstrous weight of a seemingly impersonal technology, shattered any belief amongst survivors of the inevitably beneficent nature of industrial progress.

Paradoxically, in contrast to the harsh realities of combat, modern technology in print and image was used to create a sense of illusion amongst the civilian population. As the scale of the war increased, so it became necessary to involve the whole population in active commitment to the national cause, depicted as a moral crusade. The power of propaganda to create a sense of reality all its own accounts in large measure for the unpreparedness of the German population for the shock of defeat. The exploitation of this power for both commercial and political ends was to be vigorously exploited in the post-war world.

Above all, the fact of defeat, and the collapse of the Second Empire in its turbulent aftermath, followed by the vengeful peace settlement imposed by the victors, together with the changes brought about during the conflict, meant that life in German society could not return to what it had been before 1914.

Few mourned the passing of the Empire and many celebrated its fall. In 1920 Alfred Döblin wrote: 'Remember the time of the Wilhelmine regime. Not the fabulous boom, with which the dynasty had nothing to do. Think of the Siegesallee. Of the ostentation of the *parvenus*. Of the byzantine emptiness and falsity of the spectacle and of the theatricality of the parades ... The growing apathy of the bourgeoisie, which became divided into profiteers, lickspittles, the apathetic and the discontented. The brooding atmosphere of this empire of money-grubbers, in which, from time to time, there sounded the rattling of sabres or the music of waltzes. This monstrouness, which sucked in even the working masses.'[186]

Döblin's savagery overlooked the genuine commitment and attainment of the period in his sweeping polemic. Much of this was despite the regime, even in opposition to it. In the applied arts, remarkable changes had been effected in both theory and practice, which transformed the status of Germany from the debacle of the Vienna exhibition of 1873, to the widely acknowledged centre of European leadership in this sphere of activity. Between the extremes of *völkisch* revivalism and utopian fantasy, the problems of and values appropriate to mechanization and the role of industry in modern culture, had been addressed. Although the resultant compromises blunted the rhetoric and radical aesthetics, there was a genuine if limited progress in practical terms, that was subsequently capable of extension in range and social accessibility. The results were perhaps modest when compared to the grandeur of the larger aims proclaimed by cultural reformers at various times, but it is perhaps from such small increments over a longer period, founded on consistent values having widespread acceptance, that substantial progress is achieved, rather than from dramatic transformations in pursuit of particularist ideals.

Notes

The following abbreviations have been used in the notes for journals that are repeatedly cited:

DB — Deutsche Bauzeitung

DK — Dekorative Kunst

DKuD — Deutsche Kunst und Dekoration

ID — Innendekoration

Chapter 1

1 The leading exponent of this theory of a thread in German history and character which led inevitably to National Socialism was the French historian Edmond Vermeil in, for example, *Germany's Three Reichs*, London, 1944. For a brief summary of differing interpretations on this subject see Bracher K. D. *The German Dictatorship*, Harmondsworth, 1973, pp. 15-20.

2 Quoted in Heller E., *Thomas Mann: The Ironic German*, Cleveland, 1961, pp. 148-9.

3 Frühauf, J. 'Das Kunstindustrie-Gewerbe seit dem Krieg' in *Kunst und Gewerbe*, 1875, pp. 329-31.

Chapter 2

4 Lessing J. *Das Kunstgewerbe aus der Wiener Welt-ausstellung 1873*, Berlin, 1874 pp. 4-5.

5 *Ibid* p. 53.

6 *Ibid* p. 11.

7 *Ibid* pp. 235-6.

8 *Ibid* p. 236.

9 Quoted in Waentig H., *Wirtschaft und Kunst*, Jena, 1909, p. 264.

10 'Aus der deutschen Kunst- und Kunstindustrie-Austellung in München' in *Kunst und Gewerbe*, 1876, p. 305.

11 *Ibid* p. 305.

12 'Das Eisen auf der Kunstgewerbe-Ausstellung in München 1876' in *DB*, 1876, pp. 357-8.

13 Mothes O., *Deutsches Kunstgewerbe und der Münchner Congress*, Leipzig, 1876, p. 15.

14 *Ibid* p. 21.

15 *Ibid* pp. 13-4.

16 *Ibid* p. 27.

17 *Ibid* p. 31.

18 'Versammlung deutscher Künstler, Kunstindustriellen und "Freunde derselben" zu München' in *DB*, 1876, p. 411.

19 Waentig, *Wirtschaft und Kunst*, p. 268.

20 Lessing J. *Die Renaissance im heutigen Kunstgewerbe*, Berlin, 1877, p. 22.

21 *Ibid* p. 31.

Chapter 3

22 *DB*, 1887, p. 35. The series on furniture was by Dr Peter Jessen, later to be Chief Librarian of the Berlin Museums and editor of the German Werkbund Yearbooks.

23 *Anon. Das Hamburgische Museum für Kunst und Gewerbe*, Hamburg, 1902, p. 27.

24 See *DB* Jg. XXV, Nos 43 and 45, pp. 259-60 and 270-1, for a report on the development of applied art schools in Prussia 1883-1890.

25 *Ibid*.

26 Ibid.

27 Pabst A. 'Die deutsch-nationale Kunstgewerbeausstellung in München 1888' in *Kunstgewerbeblatt*, 1889, p. 17.

28 *Ibid* pp. 17-21.

29 Luthmer F. 'Das Rococo in der heutigen Kunst' in von Salvisberg P. (ed.), *Chronik der Deutsch-Nationalen Kunstgewerbeausstellung in München 1888*, Munich, 1888, pp. 6-8.

30 *Ibid* p. 66.

31 Seliger M., 'M. Meurer's "Vergleichende Formenlehre der Pflanze"' in *DKuD*, 1909, pp. 221-3.

32 Quoted in Deneke B. 'Volkskunst und Stilwende' in Bott G. (ed.), *Von Morris zum Bauhaus*, Hanau, 1977, pp. 104-5. This has even been interpreted as a demand for 'a national art based on machine-work'. See Nerdinger W. 'Riemerschmid's Weg vom Jugendstil zum Werkbund' in Nerdinger W. (ed.), *Richard Riemerschmid vom Jugendstil zum Werkbund*, Munich, 1982, p. 23, note 73.

33 Bötticher G., 'Zu Julius Lessing's Aufsatz "Das Arbeitsgebiet des Kunstgewerbes"' in *Kunstgewerbeblatt*, 1889, pp. 124-5.

34 Masur G. *Imperial Berlin*, London, 1970, p. 101.

35 Lessing J 'Gold und Silber', a handbook for the royal museums of Berlin, 1907, quoted in Hansen H. J. (ed.) *Late Nineteenth Century Art*, Newton Abbot, 1973, p. 184.

36 Schleuning, W., 'Das Mannesmann-Rohr in seiner Bedeutung für das Kunstgewerbe' in *DB*, 1891, p. 425.

Chapter 4

37 For an account of the development of functional concepts in Germany see Müller S, *Kunst und Industrie*, Munich, 1974.

38 Heller E., *The Disinherited Mind*, Harmondsworth, 1961, p. 102.

39 Stern F. *The Politics of Cultural Despair*, New York, 1965, p. 3.

40 Langbehn J. *Rembrandt als Erzieher*, Leipzig, 1890, p. 15.

41 *Ibid* p. 17.

42 *Ibid* p. 35.

43 *Ibid* p. 27.

44 *Ibid* p. 190.

45 *Ibid* p. 191.

46 *Ibid* p. 1.

47 *Ibid* p. 191.

48 *Ibid* p. 192.

49 *Ibid* p. 210.

50 *Ibid* p. 230.

51 *Ibid* p. 273.

Chapter 5

52 Lichtwark A., 'Die Kunst in der Schule', a lecture to an educational association in Hamburg, March 1887, printed in Mannhardt W. (ed.), *Alfred Lichtwark: Eine Auswahl seiner Schriften*', Berlin, 1917, p. 36.

53 *Ibid* p. 33.

54 Quoted in Breuer G., 'Geschmacksveredelung am Ort' in exhibition catalogue *Der Westdeutsche Impuls 1900-1914: Von der Kunstlerseide zür Industriephotographie. Das Museum zwischen Jugendstil und Werkbund*, Krefeld, 1984, p. 24.

55 Lichtwark A. 'Selbsterziehung' (1896) in Mannhardt (*op.cit.*) p. 145.

56 Lichtwark, 'Die Kunst in der Schule' in Mannhardt (*op.cit.*) p. 48.

57 Quoted in Stern F. (*op.cit.*), p. 220.

58 *The Studio*, 1898, pp. 203-4.

59 *DKuD*, 1897-8, p. 140.

60 *The Studio*, 1902, p. 219.

61 'Der III allgemeine deutsche Kunstgewerbetag' in *DB*, 1896, p. 299.

62 See Kratzch G., *Kunstwart und Dürerbund*, Gottingen, 1969.

63 See Otto C. F. 'Modern Environment and Historical Continuity: The Heimatschutz Discourse in Germany' in *Art Journal*, Summer 1983, pp. 148-157.

64 Weese A. 'Hans E. v. Berlepsch-Munchen', in *DKuD*, 1899, p. 5.

65 Keyssner G. 'The Munich International Art Exhibition, in *The Studio*, 1897, p. 193.

66 *The Studio*, 1898, p. 194.

67 Weese A. (*op.cit.*) p. 1.

68 Schulze O. 'Kunstgewerbliche Arbeiten in Kayzerzinn' in *DKuD*, 1899, pp. 245-60.

69 'An die deutschen Kunstler und Kunstfreunde', editorial in *DKuD*, 1897/8, pp. I-II.

70 Schliepmann H., 'Nationale Kunst – Nothwendige Kunst', in *DKuD*, 1897/8, pp. 25-38.

71 'Erste Kunst- und Kunstgewerbeausstellung 1898 in Darmstadt' in *DKuD*, 1899, pp. 105-114.

72 Heuss T. *Erinnerungen 1903-1933*, Tubingen, 1963, p. 157-8.

73 Quoted in von Wersin W. (ed) *Deutsche Werkstätten – Möbel*, 1936, n.p.

74 Schumann, P. 'Dresdner Werkstätten für Handwerkskunst', *DK*, 1899/1900, pp. 4-5.

Chapter 6

75 'Die Vereinigte Werkstätten für Kunst im Handwerk zu München' in *DK*, 1899, p. 429.

76 Quoted in: Sternberger D., 'Panorama des Jugendstils' in *Ein Dokument Deutscher Kunst Darmstadt 1901-1976, Bd. 1*, Exhibition Catalogue published by Hessisches Landesmuseum, Darmstadt, 1976, p. 9.

77 Koch A., 'Die Darmstadter Kunstler-Kolonie', *DKuD*, 1899, p. 412.

78 Fred W., (pseudonym of Alfred Wechsler) 'The Darmstadt Artists' Colony' in *The Studio*, 1902, p. 28.

89 *Ibid* p. 29.

80 *Ibid* p. 271.

81 Hoffman A., 'Das Kunstlerische Ergebnis des Darmstadter "Dokumentes"' in *DB*, 1902.

82 *Ibid*.

83 *Ibid*.

84 *Ibid*.

85 Marchlewski J., 'Moderne Kunstströmungen und Sozialismus' in *Sezession und Jugendstil*, Dresden, 1974, p. 6.

86 *Ibid* p. 10.

87 *Ibid* p. 14.

88 'Das Kunstgewerbe oder die angewandte Kunst' in *Ibid*, p. 60.

89 *Ibid* p. 62.

90 *Ibid* p. 62.

Chapter 7

91 Quoted in Dube W-D, *The Expressionists*, London, 1972, pp. 157-8.

92 Mourey G., 'Round the Exhibition — III. "German Decorative Art"' in *The Studio*, 1901, pp. 44-50.

93 Fuchs G., 'Die Vorhalle zum Hause der Macht und der Schönheit' in *DKuD*, 1902-3, p. 6.

94 'The International Exhibition of Modern Decorative Art at Turin. The German Section' in *The Studio*, 1903, p. 194.

95 Oliver M. 'German Arts and Crafts at the St Louis Exposition' in *The Studio*, 1905, p. 233.

96 Muthesius H. 'Die Wohnungskunst auf der Welt-Austellung in St Louis' in *DKuD*, 1904-5, p. 209.

97 Volbehr T. 'Die Magdeburger Grüppe in St Louis 1904' in *DKuD*, 1904, p. 492.

98 Quoted in Carstanjen F. 'Kunstgewerbliche Erziehung' in *DKuD*, 1905, p. 478.

99 *Ibid* p. 491.

100 Quoted in Moeller G., 'Kunstgewerbeschule' in catalogue, *Der Westdeutsche Impuls 1900-1914: Kunst und Umweltgestaltung im Industriegebiet*, Düsseldorf, 1984, p. 40.

101 von Bode W., *Mein Leben*, Bd II, Berlin, 1930, p. 183.

102 Deubner L. 'Decorative Art at the Munich Exhibition' in *The Studio*, 1909, p. 42.

103 The statement was by Jules Huret, quoted in: Troy N., 'Towards a Redefinition of Tradition in French Design' in *Design Issues*, Fall 1984, p. 62.

104 Rupert Carabin, quoted in *Ibid*, p. 63.

105 Schmidt K. 'Die Ausstellung von Darstellung bauer-licher Kunst und Bauweise aus dem Konigreich Sachsen auf der Brühl'schen Terrasse in Dresden' in *DB*, 1901, pp. 253-4.

106 'Handwerker und Neuere Kunst' in *ID*, 1907, p. 51.

107 Schloermann 'Gedanken u. Vorschläge zur Innen-Einrichtung moderner Kriegs- und Handels-Schiffe in *ID*, 1907, p. 255.

108 Quoted in Wichmann H., *Aufbruch zum neuen Wohnen*, Basel and Stuttgart, 1978, p. 109.

109 Hoffman A., 'Die elektrische Hoch- und Unter-grundbahn in Berlin von Siemens und Halske, in *DB*, 1902, pp. 265-9.

110 'Studio Talk' in *The Studio*, 1907, p. 232.

Chapter 8

111 Dawson W. H., *Industrial Germany*, London and Glasgow, 1913, p. 89-91.

112 *Ibid* p. 118.

113 *Ibid* see Chapter 1, 'Population and Occupations', pp. 7-20.

114 *Ibid* p. 236.

115 Gronert S. 'Das Schöne und die Ware' in *Der Westdeutsche Impuls 1900-1914, Kunst und Umwelt-gestaltung im Industriegebiet*, Exhibition catalogue, Folkwang Museum, Essen, 1984, pp. 96-142.

116 'German Central Electricity Plant' in *The Electrical Review*, 1905, p. 631.

117 'The German Electrical Industry' in *The Electrical Review*, 1907, p. 428.

118 'Germany's Exports of Electrical Goods in 1907' in *The Electrical Review*, 1907, pp. 461-2.

119 'Commercial Attaches for German Consulates' in *The Electrical Review*, 1907, pp. 533.

120 'Atelier Nachrichten' in *DKuD*, 1898, p. 374.

121 See Gronert S., *op. cit.*

122 *The Studio*, Vol. 43, 1908, p. 151.

123 Singer H. W., 'Some New Porcelain by the Royal Saxon Factory at Meissen', *The Studio*, Vol. 40, 1907, p. 55.

124 *Ibid* pp. 56-7.

125 Gronert S., *op. cit.*

126 Stukenbrock August, *Illustrierte Hauptkatalog*, 1912. Reprinted Heidelberg 1973.

127 A. Koch, 'Kunstler, Fabrikant und Publikum' in *ID*, 1906, p. 177.

Chapter 9

128 Morris W. 'News from Nowhere' in Briggs A., *William Morris: Selected Designs and Writings*, Harmonds-worth, 1962, p. 221.

129 Schaefer K. 'Die moderne Raumkunst im Dienste des Norddeutschen Lloyd' in *ID*, 1907, p. 296.

130 Quoted from the *Fachblatt für Holzarbeiter* 1909, in Günther S., *Das Deutsche Heim*, Giessen, 1984, p. 54.

131 Breuer R. 'Der "George Washington" ' in *ID*, 1909, p. 339.

132 *Ibid* pp. 339-340.

133 Paul B., 'Passagierdampfer und ihre Einrichtungen' in *Der Verkehr*, third yearbook of the German Werkbund, Jena, 1914, pp. 55-8.

134 *Ibid* pp. 57-8.

135 *Ibid* p. 58.

136 Wichmann H., *Aufbruch zum neuen Wohnen*, Basel, 1978, p. 149.

Chapter 10

137 An abridged version of Naumann's Dresden address can be found in exhibition catalogue, *Zwischen Kunst und Industrie*, Munich, 1975, pp. 37-8

138 *Ibid*.

139 From advance pamphlet *Das dritte deutsche Kunstgewerbeausstellung* published by the organizers, probably in 1905, unpaginated. Copy in the Sächsisches Landesbibliothek, Dresden.

140 *Ibid*.

141 Rossler D., 'Von Dresdener Architektur und Kunstgewerbe vor der Ausstellung' in *DK*, 1906, p. 225.

142 Quoted in Hoffman A. 'Die Baukunst auf der dritten deutschen Kunstgewerbe-Ausstellung in Dresden 1906' in *DB*, 1906, p. 496.

143 *Ibid* p. 523.

144 Schumann P., 'Die dritte Deutsche Kunstgewerbe-Ausstellung 1906' in *Kunstgewerbeblatt*, NF 1906, pp. 165-177.

145   Naumann F. in *Zwischen Kunst und Industrie, op. cit.*, pp. 37-8.

146   Muthesius H., 'Das Maschinenmöbel' in *Dresdener Hausgerät*, 1906, quoted in Wichmann, *op cit*, p. 59.

147   Schumann, *op cit*, p. 177.

148   Günther, *op cit*, pp. 86-7.

149   Zimmermann E., 'Was Nun. Betrachtungen nach schluss der Dresdener Kunstgewerbe Ausstellung', in *DKuD*, 1906/7, p. 172.

150   'Deutscher Volkunst und Volkskundetag zu Dresden 1906' in *DB*, 1906, pp. 564-5.

151   Zimmermann, *op cit*, p. 172.

152   Muthesius H., 'Die Bedeutung des Kunstgewerbes' in catalogue, *Zwischen Kunst und Industrie*, Munich, 1975, pp. 39-50.

153   Dietz M., 'Neuzeitliche Kunst-Bestrebungen in Würtemburg, in *DKuD*, 1907, pp. 117-163.

154   'Eine Beachtenswerte Antwort' in *DKuD*, 1907, pp. 164-5.

155   See Osborn M., 'Der Deutsche Kunstgewerbekrieg' in *Kunstgewerbeblatt*, NF 1907, pp. 189-191.

156   Bruckmann P., 'Die Grundung des deutschen Werkbundes' in *Zwischen Kunst und Industrie, op cit*, pp. 25-30.

Chapter 11

157   The artists were Peter Behrens, Theodor Fischer, Josef Hoffman, Wilhelm Kreis, Max Läuger, Adelbert Niemayer, Josef-Maria Olbrich, Bruno Paul, Richard Riemerschmid, J. J. Scharvogel, Paul Schultze-Naumburg and Fritz Schumacher. The overlap with the twelve firms is in many cases obvious: P Bruckmann und Söhne, Deutsche Werkstätten, Dresden, Eugen Diederichs, Kunstdruckerei Künstlerbund Karlsruhe, Gebr. Klingspor, Poeschel and Trepte, Saalecker Werkstätten, Vereinigte Werkstätten, Munich, Werkstätten für deutschen Hausrat Theophil Müller Dresden, Wiener Werkstätten, Wilhelm and Co., Gottlob Wünderlich.

158   The above list and Schumacher's address are both given in 'Zur Grundungsgeschichte des Deutschen Werkbundes' in *Die Form*, No. 11, 1932, reprinted in *Zwischen Kunst und Industrie, op cit*, pp. 30-34.

159   The quotations in the two paragraphs above are from 'Der Deutsche Werkbund: Denkschrift des Ausschusses 1907' in *Zwischen Kunst und Industries*, pp. 50-55.

160   Müller S, *Kunst und Industrie*, Munich 1974, see the section *Funktionalismus und normative Ästhetik*, p. 37ff.

161   Muthesius H. 'Wo Stehen wir?' in *Zwischen Kunst und Industrie*, p. 60.

162   Muthesius H., 'Das Formproblem im Ingenieurbau', *Ibid*, p. 76.

163   *Ibid* p. 78.

164   *Ibid* p. 77.

165   'Wo Stehen wir? *Ibid*, p. 60.

166   *Ibid*, p. 64. See also Muthesius' conclusions to the discussion following his address, p. 65.

167   Lux J. A. 'Das Kunstlerische Problem der Industrie' in *ID*, 1908, pp. 81-109. This was later printed as a chapter in Lux, *Das Neue Kunstgewerbe in Deutschland*, Leipzig, 1908.

168   Lux J. A. 'Nationalität und Amerikanismus' in *ID*, 1908, pp. 275-9.

169   van der Velde H., 'Kunst und Industrie' in *Zwischen Kunst und Industrie*, p. 59.

170   Breuer R., 'Typus und Individualität' *DKuD*, 1914, p. 378.

171   Quoted in Buddensieg T. and Rogge H., *Industriekultur: Peter Behrens und die AEG, 1907-1914*, Berlin, 1979, p. 44.

172   Jaumann A., 'Neues von Peter Behrens' in *DKuD*, 1908-9, pp. 343-57.

173   From a report of Behrens' speech reprinted in Buddensieg and Rogge, *op cit*, p. D276.

174   *Ibid* p. D276.

175   *Ibid* p. D276.

176   'Kunst und Technik' in Buddensieg and Rogge, p. D279. Houston Stewart Chamberlain was born in Britain, but grew up in Germany, taking German nationality and marrying a daughter of Richard Wagner. Chamberlain became a leading exponent of the more extreme tenets of *völkisch* ideology.

177   *Ibid* pp. D278-285.

178   Pogge von Strandmann H. *Walther Rathenau: Industrialist, Banker, Intellectual and Politician. Notes and Diaries 1907-1922*, Oxford, 1985.

179   Jaumann A., 'Die wirtschaftliche Bedeutung des deutschen Kunstgewerbes' in *ID*, 1907, pp. 338-344.

180   Westheim P., 'Soziale Verplichtung des Kunstgewerblers' in *DKuD*, 1909/10, pp. 143-6.

181   'Der gedekte Tisch' in *Kunstwart*, March 1912, p. 334.

182   Schoenfelder-Elberfeld 'Hygiene und Innen-Kunst' in *ID*, 1906, pp. 208-9.

Chapter 13

183   Hellmich W. 'Zehn Jahre deutscher Normung' in *DIN 1917-1927*, Berlin, 1927, p. 8.

184   von Bode W., 'Ein Wendepunkt der Entwicklung der deutschen Kunst' in *ID*, 1915, p. 33.

185   Muthesius H., 'The Future of German Form' in Benton T. and C. with Sharp D., *Form and Function*, London 1975, p. 56.

186   Quoted in Craig G., *Germany 1866-1945*, Oxford, 1981, p. 338.